PEOPLE'S LIBRARY MOVEMENT

A meagre offering
at the feet of Divine Mother
Sri Mookambika
in all humilitv

ABOUT THE AUTHOR

Prof. R. Raman Nair took his Master Degree in Library and Information Science from Banaras Hindu University and Bachelor of Laws and MA History from University of Kerala. He has worked in Centre for Development Studies. Trivandrum Public Library, Cochin University of Science and Technology, Kerala Legislature Library, Government PG College at Kasaragod, and Maharajas College for Women at Trivandrum. Presently he is the Librarian of Kerala Agricultural University.

He has designed the Multimeda Library Automation System (McLAS 1993) and also the Building LAN of KAU Library which is one of the largest multmedia library and informaton systems in the country. He has 14 books which includes *Public Library Development, Computer Application to Library and Information Services,* and *Internet for Library and Information Services,* 120 research papers and articles and many national and international conference presentations to his credit. He has organised various seminars and conferences including the *National Seminar on Right to Information* and All India IASLIC Conference 1998.

Prof. Nair has associated with many expert committees formed by professional organizations, universities and government. He is a research fellow of American Biographical Institute and is the founder member of Centre for South Indian Studies, life member of Rural Development Forestry Network (ODI, London), Asian Watershed Management Network (Katmandu, Nepal), ILA, IASLIC and AGLIS. In recognition of the support provided by him for diffusing geographic knowledge and promoting research and exploration; the Board of Trustees of National Geographic Society (Washington) have also enrolled him as its member.

PEOPLE'S LIBRARY MOVEMENT

PROF. R. RAMAN NAIR
University Librarian
Kerala Agricultural University
Trichur -680654

CONCEPT PUBLISHING COMPANY, NEW DELHI - 110059

ISBN 81-7022-822-0

First Published 2000

Published and Printed by
Ashok Kumar Mittal
Concept Publishing Company
A/15-16, Commercial Block, Mohan Garden,
NEW DELHI - 110059 (India)

Phones : 5648039, 5649024
Fax : 091-(11)-5648053
E-mail : publishing@conceptpub.com

PREFACE

Progress in all walks of life depends on information generated in the concerned spheres, upto the present. The availability of information, expeditiously and pin pointedly, supports decision making processes at all levels. Relevant information accelerates the pace of national development. An informed citizen is an asset to a democratic system of government. Proper utilization of information by a democratic system can improve the quality of life and activities of the citizens. So, ready access to information generated by society and accumulated through time is a fundamental right of every citizen. It should be ensured by sound legislation. Public library is the only effective social repository which can collect and organize information and provide access to it to all people in an equal and unbiased way.

The present explosive nature of the production of recorded information and the direct relation of information to developments in all spheres of human life emphasizes the need to give more priority to the planning of systems which deal with this basic resource. In a federal country like India if total information resources of the nation is to be pooled together and equally shared between constituent States; information systems are to be planned at national levels. The Government of India has realized the value of co-ordinating and upgrading the library and information systems at national level. Result was the forming of Raja Rammohun Roy Library Foundation, Chattopadhyaya Committee for formulating National Policy on Library and Information Systems, and initiating of programmes like NISSAT, NICNET, ERNET, ARIS, INFLIBNET etc.

To enable the States to share the results of these programmes; the library and information systems maintained by all the States should have a uniform pattern. Without that State level systems cannot become active parts of a coherent whole, that is the national system. The State library systems also should be based upon sound legislation according to a pattern suggested by the Centre.

In India at present there is no national level public library system or legislation. Among the States only a few have enacted library legislation. But they have followed no uniform pattern or they envisage any national level co-ordination. Their working shows that they are not at all effective. Most of the remaining States are also at present seriously thinking about enacting library legislation. According to the present trend most of them may come out with defective legislation. This will make it difficult to bring these State systems into line and materialize a National Library and Information System. The objectives of optimum utilization of resources, efficient service and equal access to information will remain unattainable. So a serious and pragmatic thinking on State library legislation requires special attention at this time.

In this treatise an attempt is made to study the public library development in Kerala, a State with a glorious history of library movement which has also enacted a library legislation. The library movement, attempts for library legislation and the resultant Public Library Act is evaluated in detail.

The approach to the subject is entirely new. Instead of simply giving a narration of what happened and when in a chronological order; or comparing the system and legislation with other similar ones or some suggested models; the history of the movement for library legislation and the evolution of the library law through various stages and the influences through time and space which finally got deposited in the legislation are analysed. An understanding of all these are required to fully apprehend and evaluate a library movement and resultant system and legislation. No previous study on library movement has taken such an approach.

This study also identified five roughly divided periods or phases in the development of the library movements, systems and legislations. They being stages of evolution can be applied to the study of this subject in general or in limits of any aspect or geographical region.

This study identifies the historical and socio-political trends that may cause defective library system and enactment of unappropriate library legislation. It also points out the measures to prevent the enactment of defective library legislation. But unlike many studies which approach State library acts as independent ones here it is viewed as a constituent part of a whole, that is National Act.

The subject; library movement and library legislation is of importance and interest to common man who would like to know the process which shaped the institution known as public library, the system and the law which is to maintain his right for access to information accumulated by the society. Among the expected readers of this topic, the number of rural library workers, social activists and public library users to whom this book may also be of interest will be hundreds of times greater than library scientists, historians and other academicians. To provide more, readability for the common man the structure of this work is kept very simple and too much technicality in language and plan of the work is avoided. The traditional method of defining the subject at the beginning is purposefully not followed to define the institution at the stage when the concept is fully developed.

Each chapter deals with a particular phase or aspect of the subject in a separate but not necessarily self-contained way. The First Chapter gives a general introduction and substantiate the method in which the topic is dealt here. In the next chapter an attempt has been made to outline the cultural, educational, economic and environmental setting in which the developments of our concern took place. The subsequent five chapters (3 to 7) analyse the library movement and evolution of library systems and laws of the region through their first four phases of the five identified by this study. The developments of the outside world which influenced and contributed to the growth of this institution in Kerala have been traced in Chapter Eight. In Chapter Nine the goals and objectives of public library are discussed. Chapter Ten and Eleven discusses the fifth phase of library movement that is the present one. In Chapter Twelve the concept of modern library system and principles of library legislation accepted all over the world in the present phase, which are to be the measuring rods for evaluating the objectives of any library movement as well as the resultant library system and law are described.

In Chapter thirteen, an analysis, discussion and comparison of the Kerala Public Libraries Act 1989, is done in the light of the ideals expressed in Chapters Nine and Twelve and the Model Act prepared by Dr. S.R. Ranganathan and also the other existing State Acts. On the basis of the strength and weakness of the Act brought to light, recommendations for amendments in the act and suggestions for preventing the enactment of defective legislation at other States in future, are put forward in the concluding chapter.

This work is an attempt to make a modest beginning for study in a further largely untried field–a critical analysis of the history of the library movement of a particular area and also the comparative analysis of the library legislation which is one of the important achievement of the movement. This can enable identifying the diseased trends in library movements which may result in the defective end products. The study also recommends amendments for rectifying the defects in legislation and suggest measures to avoid the enactment of defective legislation in other regions in future.

No comprehensive investigation on this line into the library movement in India or any of the library legislations existing in our States has been made earlier and if this study could infuse interest for detailed study of other State library movements and existing State library legislations this book will serve more than its purpose.

For infusing into me an interest to prepare a full length work on this topic in which I have been writing articles mainly in Malayalam for a long time; for giving me the confidence to work on it; for patiently helping me to correct, polish and strengthen my views expressed here; I am indebted to Dr. S.N. Singh, Department of Library and Information Science, Banaras Hindu University.

I am grateful to Sri C.R. Sathikumar of Library, Research and Reference Division of Kerala Legislature and Sri N.K. Bhagi, Editor, International Library Movement, Ambala, Haryana who have connected me with rare source materials on the topic and to Sri Jasbeer Singh, Zoological Survey of India Library, Patna, who helped me for preparing the final manuscript due to his love towards me and his interest in the topic. The book was prepared during my stay at Varanasi. The comforts of their home many have shared with me in Kashi transcending the cultural and linguistic barriers and the homeliness, and peace Holy Kashi has given to me are more than that to be expressed in mere words.

What is good and original in this work became possible due to the help and strength which came to me from all these sources.

R. RAMAN NAIR

CONTENTS

1

INTRODUCTION

Society's need of initiating as it were its younger members into a definite state of knowledge seems to reach back into man's biological past[1]. It is this motive that led to the invention of writing which can communicate knowledge through space and time, and in the birth of the institution which is to store and disseminate the accumulated knowledge of society for its members.

The existence of and access to such social accumulation of knowledge is of utmost significance in the relationship it establishes between society and its single members. Society has to transmit to the individual a required portion of knowledge in the interest of common welfare. Any member should also be able to draw at will the required knowledge from the store of knowledge. Unless this accumulated knowledge is active in society an individual will not be able to perform his due function as a member of society and contribute positively to the welfare of society. So the society will not be able to conduct its communal life on the highest level which is actually possible.

Society expects man to be self-governing, truth loving, informed, generous, tolerant, reverent, a champion of freedom, a citizen of the world, aware of beauty and desirous of leaving the world better for his stay in it[2]. To serve these purposes collections of recorded knowledge existed in all ages of human history as a part of the social fabric. When we consider such high expectations of society in respect of man as an individual we realize the full potential of library, the only social institution which procure, preserve and transfer information and knowledge for the advancement of society. Throughout history society was aware of this potentiality and so library existed as a most important social institution in all ages.

Social Movement

Library Science is a social science and librarianship is ultimately social in its purpose[3]. According to Maurice B. Line librarianship is a communication between knowledge and society. To study any aspect of library science, methods and techniques borrowed from the social sciences are required[4]. Library being such a social institution the legislation related to it is a social legislation. All social systems are the result of unending evolution, which extends over centuries, which derives their factors from; its different stages and systems, the common traditions and customs and laws and decrees passed by rulers in different ages to make the institution more useful to greatest possible numbers.

So library movement and library legislation of a particular region can be fully apprehended and evaluated only through an understanding and analysis of the influences that reached it through time and space. It is this motivation and not an interest in the antequarian or the curious that supports the importance given in this treatise to the historical analysis of the development of the library system, and movement for library legislation in Kerala.

Need for Historical Analysis

If history teaches us anything; says Raymond Irvin, it is that life is a constant succession of turning points, each in some sort a legacy of the past, and none of them more decisive in reality than any others. A knowledge of what has happened in the past is essential if we would progress into the future, avoiding the mistakes of our predecessors, adopting methods that have proved successful and pursuing paths that have been blazed for our guidance with the object of extending them further towards our goal[5]. But still library history suffers from the rigid limitations of many centuries of conventional chronicling which were only quantitative descriptions and are foundations of library history and not history in any enlightened modern sense[6]. But recently we find in James Thompson, Kathryn McChesney etc. champions of its liberation into full dignity of recognition as an integral expression of social forces. With them we can believe a new phase has dawned for the study of library history.

The history of a subject should form the basic ingredient of its study. It need not be intensive, but should commence as a general survey of the entire field with a closer look at the most significant events. In library legislation this enables one to respect the antiquity of our calling, to appreciate the gradual advance and sometimes decline of various movements and systems, and to base our future on sound foundations. We can take advantage of past experience, and learn from the mistakes of others instead of repeating them.

So long is the time span covered by libraries and the rules and laws related to that social institution, that it must follow that the main principles of library legislation are now exceptionally well established[7]. Only the most ignorant individual would, in professional terms set out to reinvent the wheel[8]. Conversely it also follows that any librarian or legislator, even in apparently the most contemporary situations, will always benefit from a return to earlier principles[9]. It is after all a fact that we base our lives on previous experience, and can predict our future only on the basis of past performance. All good workers appreciate that they stand on the shoulders of other. They are grateful for what their more primitive predecessors have done and could perform their own tasks more intelligently and efficiently if they have studied the stages in the development of their art[10]. So Lawrence S. Thompson goes as far as to consider library history as an invaluable aid to future generations in their attempt to avoid the errors of the past[11].

Occultations in Evolution

While it remains true that librarians must build upon the experience of their own past; it is unfortunately equally true that the development of libraries and librarianship has not been some kind of evolutionary process whereby these have grown better and better. Some primitive predecessors' were very much more effective in what they did than many of their successors; and it is not only from the errors of the past that a librarian can learn, but from the neglected and unacknowledged triumphs also. It appears as often as not that our predecessors in their own terms knew the true path. This view point expressed very clearly and accurately by D.M. Norris is relevant to library legislation also[12]. The term history suggests rather an evolutionary or gradual development, but such is not the case with library movement, knowledge dissemination systems, and rules and laws related to that. The ancient were proficient in the art as we are today, but their methods were different[13]. So it is, throughout the ages and therefore it is not a history, but a survey of the different concepts systems and rules.

A more perceptive view about the historical analysis of library systems, legislations and concepts is offered by E.A. Savage. He propounds a theory of 'occultations'. Observing that since the technology of library systems and legislations is limited and narrow, an enthusiastic librarian or legislator diligently searches for new ideas, but rarely discovers any[14]. The open shelf is the oldest of ideas. The chief concepts of library system undergo periodical occultations. They emerge again the brighter for the eclipse and shine upon us for a time, and fade again into obscurity. We lose ideas, regain them, fight against them, yield to them and forget them once more[15].

The chapters of this treatise devoted to historical analysis in effect trace the waxings and wanings of at least the major principles which have characterised library system and library movement in Kerala. Good principles can be seen to be good principles on the basis of comparative analysis and factual evidence. Like this bad principles are equally and similarly identifiable. In this analysis we find that in Kerala, the movement for library legislation and library development has followed too far a wrong path, which is an odd twist given by Kerala Granthasala Sangham the dominant force which led the movement[16]. Everywhere, it is a remarkable fact that despite current and former occultations the essential principles of library systems emerge unambiguously and uncontrovertibly from our long history[17]. So in Kerala also we can hope for that. For a healthy and useful growth; library development would have to follow directions of proved advantage.

The Five Phases of Evolution

Library being a social institution, the development of libraries and the traditions, customs, rules and laws related it are inextricably connected to the social and cultural development of man[15]. In all the phases of socio-cultural development of man this knowledge disseminating institution was present and it fulfilled its role successfully. The success of any institution inaugurated and operated in the service of the community depends on three main factors: it must have purpose and its objectives clearly established, it must have a sound administration to determine its priorities and the method of putting them into practice and after the methods have been agreed they must be put into effect by capable and conscientious executives[18]. The survey of the history of library development in Kerala also indicates the existence and evolution of these factors through all ages. In socio-cultural development there have been different ages and libraries likewise have developed through different ages[19]. If we analyse the historical evolution of library systems and customs, traditions and laws related to that in Kerala we can recognize five roughly divided overlapping periods or phases. Social conditions and formats have changed over these periods but not the basic function of libraries; to collect preserve and disseminate the knowledge accumulated by society, to the members of the society for the ultimate benefit of the society.

In Kerala during the first phase this basic function was actively present and it was meant for all members of society without any restrictions. The only thing was that the institutions which undertook these functions were not named with the term library. In the second phase Kerala comes into contact with western ideas of education and libraries. The term public library was used to denote the institution which undertook the knowledge dissemination function. Influenced by British administrators and as a part of educational reforms, State established and maintained public libraries, and made rules, orders and laws required for maintaining them. In the third phase people became aware of the possibilities of this institution in political and social reform and as a result a people's library movement took birth. Government while continuing its own library development activities supported the people's movement and both got inspiration from each other. In the fourth phase the people's library movement which is headed by political and social activists who have no interest or expertise for development of library and information systems on scientific lines, structured the movement into an organization very much like a strong political party.

In the beginning of the fifth phase that is the present one which we are witnessing; the State comes into contact with the research and development on library and information dissemination systems going on in India and abroad. State accepts its responsibility for the establishment of a library and information system for the people and moves for that. Here the people's movement comes into conflict with the government. The interest of the organization; Kerala Granthasala Sangham that headed the people's movement resists the government's attempt for reform and intervention in the field it wants to dominate[20]. This delayed for more than four decades (1947-1989) government's all move to enact a library legislation in Kerala. Due to people's indifference and ignorance about modern library systems and their possibilities, and the wide support obtained by the Kerala Granthasala Sangham against government through its mass appealing shallow programmes, government was forced to make a conciliation with this movement. Result was enactment of a defective library legislation.

Sequence and Extent of Phases

The conceptual phases mentioned above are not clear-cut chronological divisions. Existence and development of a particular concept cannot be divided by boundaries of time. The same phase may continue to exist in some aspects or places even after the birth of the next phase. Each phase may overlap the other at both ends. In Kerala even after government has initiated the fifth phase the Kerala Granthasala Sangam remained in the fourth phase and opposed the fifth phase.

Human society has never shown uniform development. There have been focal points or areas of rapid growth in one region while other parts of the country remained relatively stagnant. So the different regions may not be under the same phase at a time. For example when we take India as a whole; the fifth phase starts in 1930 when S.R. Ranganathan introduced the Model Library Act at the All Asia Educational Conference convened at Benaras. The system suggested by him was far advanced than any library system existing anywhere in the world at that time. But in Kerala the phase starts in 1947 when the State requested S.R. Ranganathan to prepare a library bill and development plan for Kerala. Some other States still continue in the earlier phases.

Even the sequence or number of phases may differ. In Baroda the fifth phase was present from 1900 immediately after the second phase, and it reached its excellence when the king Sayaji Rao built up an elaborate public library system for his people. But after him again Baroda was forced to return to an earlier phase which we can identify as third one, which continued its usual course. Baroda is a very good example for the theory of occultations put forward by E.A. Savage.

REFERENCES

1. Butler, Pierce. *Introduction to Library Science.* Chicago: Phonix, 1933.
2. Mukherjee, A.K. *Librarianship: Its Philosophy and History.* Bombay, Asia, 1966.
3. Downs, Robert B. Resources for research in librarianship. *Library trends.* 1964, 13, 6 14.
4. Line, Maurice B. *Lines of Thought: Selected Papers.* London: Clive Bingley. 1988.
5. Thornton, John L. *Selected Readings in the History of librarianship.* London: Library Association. 1966.
6. Kaufman, Paul. Some community libraries in eighteenth century Europe: A reconnaissance. *Libri.* 1972, 22, 1-57.

7. Thompson, James. *History of Principles of Librarianship.* London: Clive Bingley, 1977.
8. *Ibid.*
9. *Ibid.*
10. Cashmore, H.M. In his forward to Norris, D.M. *History of Cataloguing.* London: Grafton, 1939.
11. Thompson, Lawrence S. In his preface to Predeek, A. *History of Libraries in Great Britain and America.*
12. Norris, D.M. *History of Cataloguing.* London, Grafton, 1939.
13. Raman Nair, R. Nature and use of library history. In *Library Movement and Library Development in India.* New Delhi, ILA, 1994.
14. Savage, E.A. In his introduction to Thornton, John L. *Chronology of Librarianship.* 1941.
15. *Ibid.*
16. Raman Nair, R. *Op. cit.,* 13.
17. Thompson, James. *Op. cit.,* 7.
18. Murison, W.J. *Public Library: Its Origin Purpose and Significance,* Ed. 3. London: Clive Bingley, 1988.
19. Olle, James G. *Library History.* London: Clive Bingley, 1967.
20. Raman Nair, R. Kerala Granthasala Sangham lackshyam nediyo. Cochin: *Veekshanam,* 12 August 1987.

2

ENVIRONMENTAL SETTINGS

Located in the southern extremity of the Indian subcontinent, the State of Kerala is resplendent for its scenic splendour as well as its eminent contribution to the country's intellectual and cultural landscape. It is a land where nature still holds her own inspite of industrialization, urban influx and high population; where the literacy rate is highest in the country, where people of diverse fashions and political beliefs have been able to forge a common ethos and find a common identity. Foremost among the advantages that Kerala enjoys is the abundance of educated and skilled manpower that has made its presence felt in other parts of the country as well as abroad[1].

With the southern most extremity at Parassala, about 56 kms up from the lands end of India, Kerala stretches along the shores of Arabian sea for a distance of about 580 kms with Karnataka State on the north and north-east and Tamil Nadu State on the east and south. The breadth of the State varies from 32 kms in the extreme north and south to over 120 kms in the middle. It is hemmed between the mighty Western Ghats and the Arabian sea.

The sea helped Kerala in moulding her history. The maritime tradition of the State can be traced to the hoary days of antiquity. Peaceful interaction with farflung lands through trade had built up a tradition of more than two millennia before the incursions from modern Europe symbolised by the landing of Vasco Da Gama at Calicut in 1498 changed the temper of contact, loaded it with conflicts and inflicted a turbulent phase of history which ended only with independence[2].

Throughout the past Kerala has been one of the most dynamic historical regions of India. She maintained the fundamental unity of Indian culture. Like in other fields, in education and related areas;

eventhough she developed individually in ancient period she formed the characteristic of Indian spirit and pattern[3]. When excellent achievements were attained in education and culture or when drastic changes were going on in the process of education or methods of organization and dissemination of knowledge in India; we can see the parallel development in Kerala also. But Kerala infused into everything her own individuality and thus contributed additional features to the national stream. The cultural affinities of Kerala with the rest of South India are still deeper and more intimate.

Area and Population

Kerala ranks seventeenth in area among the twenty-five States of India. The total area of the State is 38,863 sq.km. This area works out to 1.18 per cent of the total area of the country. According 1991 census, Kerala has a population of about 29,032,828 persons which is about 3 per cent of the population of India. Considering the size of the population Kerala is twelfth among the 25 States of India. With 29 million people living in a small State with an area of 38,863 sq. km., Kerala has a high density of population; 747 persons per sq. km., the all India average being 216 only[4]. This is the basic problem of Kerala. The larger the population the smaller will be the ability of the community to save and invest in developmental activities.

Constitution and Government

Pre-independence Kerala was under three separate administrative units. Travancore and Cochin were ruled by local kings and Malabar was part of the province of British Empire. Cochin State merged into Travancore in 1949 to form Travancore-Cochin State[5]. In 1956 when the Indian States were reorganized into linguistic States, whole of Malabar District and Kasaragod Taluk of South Canara District joined the other two and the present Kerala State was born[6]. Kerala became one of the States of the Indian union which is a Soverign Socialist Secular Democratic Republic. The Constitution of India which envisages parliamentary system of government is federal in structure with unitary features. The Constitution distributes the legislative power between the union legislature and the State legislature and provides for vesting of residual powers in parliament.

The Union Executive consists of the President, the Vice-President, and the council of ministers with the Prime Minister at the head to aid and advise the President. The legislature of the union called Parliament consists of the president and two houses Lok Sabha and Rajya Sabha. The main functions of the parliament are to make laws for the country and to make finances available to the government for services of the state. All legislation require the consent of the Parliament.

There are twenty-five States and seven union territories in India. Like all other States Kerala reproduced the structure of the Union government in miniature: Governor, Council of Ministers with Chief Minister at its head and Legislative Assembly. There is however no second chamber.

The Constitution divides legislative powers into three groups; union, State and concurrent of which the longest and most important is union list. State legislatures have exclusive powers over the subjects enumerated in State list. Education the most important function, so far as libraries are concerned, is reserved to the states, though there is a central Ministry of Education with co-ordinating powers, including that of making grants for specific purposes like for libraries, adult education etc. These powers have been increased by the very large sums made available under successive plans. The Central Government is responsible for the co-ordination of facilities and determination of standards in respect of higher education, research, technical and scientific education and libraries. The central government is also responsible for the operation of five universities and a few libraries of national importance.

Local Administration

Local government is in the hands of municipal authorities which have primary functions relating to their own areas and frame their own budgets, though usually however, these require approval of State government. For rural areas there is a three-tier system of Panchayats or local councils at village, block and district levels. The District is the taxing authority below the State. The system is virtually complete, and one therefore can say that the local administration proceeds from State to city, district and right down to its roots the villages.

Kerala has a rural sociology different from the rest of India. Only 26 per cent of the State's population lived in urban areas in 1991. The Governments have always tried to provide effective and well planned services to rural areas in different fields of education, library service, medical aid, water supply, electrification, housing, public distribution, communications, public transport etc. Thus the rural population does not have to migrate to towns in search of these facilities. Such fairly evenly spread infrastructure development has evidently prevented the overcrowding of cities and towns.

Education and Literacy

Kerala the most literate and educationally advanced region of India, which occupies an honoured place among States in point of educational progress, cultural advancement and literacy; has got a proud history of educational and library movements. The people's library movement which took birth in the last quarter of the nineteenth century has contributed much to the mass literacy which is Kerala's special feature. Commendable progress has been made in education, and the literacy rate has been improved by 59 per cent since 1901 while the all India increase is only 31 per cent.

The literacy in the State is above 70 per cent according to 1981 census. This high literacy rate even though is mostly minimum reading ability has enabled the newspapers to have largest circulation than their colleagues of other States. Even in 1977 there were 71 dailies published from Kerala with total 1.1 million copies of which 12 sold 8,00,000 copies. Newspaper readership is highest in the State than anywhere else in India and the habit of reading a politically informed daily paper well enough established among the lower castes and poorer classes as to render the claim that by lunch time every Malayali read his morning news[12]. To Keralites; literate or illiterate, reading or hearing the daily news read; has become a habit like coffee and cigarette. But 60 per cent of these readers are not able to afford copy of a daily newspaper and their source for that had been, far decades the reading rooms and coffee shops of the villages or village towns. It is this character that maintained and strengthened the people's library movement in Kerala. But the objectives of the libraries and reading rooms so maintained starts and ends with this minimum purpose.

Library Scene

State Government has always kept aside a good amount for maintaining libraries and reading rooms for the people. In 1987-88 and 1988-89 the expenditure for public libraries was Rs. 98.10 and Rs. 99.54 lakhs respectively[13]. The budget estimate for 1989-90 for education is Rs. 584.58 crores[14]. It comes to 40.95 per cent of the total expenditure. The budget estimate for 1989-90 for public libraries is Rs. 106.12 lakhs[15]. The slight increase in the amount which was almost static for more than half a decade would have been due to the influence of recent library legislation.

The official national language of India under the Constitution is Hindi. But under the Official Language Act of 1963 English will continue to be in use as an official language for an indefinite period alongside Hindi. In Kerala the regional language Malayalam is also taught at various levels with Hindi and English and most of the courses for study are available in Malayalam medium also. Malayalam is one of the fourteen officially recognized regional languages of India. The other languages spoken are Tamil, Kanarese, Konkani, Gujarati, Marathi, Arabic and Hebrew.

In the light of all the above facts we can see that the problems of public library provision are very great. Kerala is only a part of Indian union. The State has a predominantly rural population and a small per capita income. The most difficult problems are those arising from the local government system and the relations of the Central Government to the States. Provision of public library service is reserved to the States and it is their sole responsibility. The Central Government has no coercive powers to enforce; legislation by the States, or to dictate the form of such legislation. All these makes difficult, national level co-ordination, and flow of information from national collections to the common man through State public library system.

REFERENCES

1. Ramachandran Nair, Adoor, K.K. *Kerala State Gazetteer*. Trivandrum: State Gazetteers, 1986. Vol. 2, Part 1.
2. Kunjan Pillai, Elamkulam, P.N. Studies in Kerala History. Kottayam: *NBS*, 1970.
3. Kunjan Pillai, Elamkulam, P.N. Samskarathinte nazhikakallukal. Kottayam: *NBS*, 1960.
4. India. Census of India 1989. Series 10. *Kerala*. New Delhi: Publications Division, 1989.
5. Sredhara Menon, A. A survey of Kerala history. Kottayam: *SPCS*, 1976.
6. *Ibid.*
7. India, Information and Broadcasting, Ministry of. *India: A Reference Annual* 1987. New Delhi, Publications Division, 1987.
8. India, *Op. cit.*, 4.
9. *Ibid.*

10. India. *Op. cit.*, 7.
11. India. *Op. cit.*, 4.
12. Kerala, Public Relations, Dept. of *Press in Kerala: A Useful Summary*. Trivandrum: Government Press, 1977.
13. Kerala. Explanatory memorandum on budget for 1989-90. Trivandrum, Government Press, 1989.
14. Kerala. Kerala budget in brief, 1989-90. Trivandrum: Government Press, 1989.
15. Kerala, *Op. cit.*, 13.

3

EVOLUTION THROUGH TIME

The beginnings of libraries and the customs, traditions, rules and laws related to that social institution are lost in antiquity. With the recording of human thoughts, starts also the concept of library which preserves thoughts for future use. When our prehistoric men drew the pictures on the wall of the safest portion of their cave, or his predecessors dried clay tablets in the banks of Indus or Sumer, they were doing the same thing that our modern information scientist is doing while he moves his fingers through a key board; to feed information which is to be preserved for future use into computer memory. From primitive cave walls, medium for storing information developed through clay tablet, papyrus or parchment rolls, the illuminated manuscript, the vellum codex, the incunabula, the printed book, audio and video cassettes, microforms, culminating in the computer maintained data bases. The customs, traditions, rules and laws related to storing of information for use also has a parallel development.

When we examine the activities of libraries through time and space, we see that the basic function in which all kinds of institutions which we have to call libraries eventhough they were not known by that term were engaged is collection, preservation and dissemination of knowledge. In this sense; library and even the concept of public library is old as civilization. These ancient social institutions were libraries or public libraries not by their name but by their activities. None of the ancient libraries ever remained as mere store houses as we alleges them to be. From the time of the first prehistoric cave drawing, users always existed. The only thing is that until very recent times their numbers have been small. But the stored information was put into effective use and was always active in the society.

Origins of Free Public Libraries

Concept of public library is related to the principles of access than with those principles which govern the size, content or organization of the collections[1]. History of public access is also a long and continuous one. The theory that free public library is a relatively recent phenomenon as put forward by all the works on library history is wrong. The principle "libraries are for all" existed right down the ages. All the ancient libraries were open to everyone and evidence of public access to libraries existed continuously from earliest period of human history.

With the pre-historic man's first attempt to store information for other's use in the cave wall through pictographic inscription; customs traditions, rules and procedures related to the information storage and dissemination also took birth. These principles in an evolution through time, absorbing the influences through space, culminates in the modern concept of library system and library legislation. But we cannot equate those ancient conditions with that of the present. Ancient libraries were public libraries only in the sense that they were at the service of those who could use them and who cared to use them. But these libraries welcomed all those who really were in need of the information stored there. They have also their own traditional methods of making the user aware of the existence of his required information. There were differences between the libraries of ancient times and that of today which we call progress. But one thing we have to remember is that ancient libraries and their methods and laws suited the society that created them. In a comparison of them with our present libraries we will also find that many of the ancient libraries had huge well organized collections, efficient services were maintained from public fund, they were based on accepted laws, and were better than the best libraries that are within the reach of the 75 per cent of our people in the present days.

Library starts with the recording of thoughts. The oldest system of writing known to us is the cuneiform and the people of Sumeria and Indus Valley practised this as early as 3000 BC. Thousands of clay tablets in which they recorded their religious thoughts, details of rituals, legends, lores and communications related to trade and commerce were excavated from Sumeria and Indus Valley. They constitute man's oldest literature and in both of these civilizations huge collections of records existed. The attempts for the decipherment of Indus script reveals that; preserved in the Indus seals and tablets were the social, political and philosophical thinking of that people. It has been recorded from Sumeria's ancient cities that; by 2700 BC they have a lot of document collections and the one at Tello was reputed to have 30,000 clay tablets[2].

Ancient Egypt also had a number of libraries. A very big library existed at Gizeh in 2500 BC and about 1250 BC Ramses II established a library at Thebes and at its entrance he inscribed ''medicine for soul'' which proves it is open to all.

Awareness of Government's Responsibility

The most important and largest efficient collection in the ancient world was established by Assyrian king Assurbanipal at Nineveh in seventh century BC[3]. His library contained more than 20,000 clay tablets besides a huge collection of leather scrolls and papyri. He undertook a systematic collection of all recorded information—religious, historical, geographical and scientific knowledge from all parts of the known world. They were classified catalogued and arranged in the most useful order. The plan of library, the specialized equipments and staff and the liberal provision for the use of stock are not attained so perfectly even in the present day by most of our public libraries. According to Jules Oppert the Assyriologist of last century Assurbanipal had expressly prepared this large collection for the purpose of instruction of his subjects and his collection of documents was open to all the people[4]. Here we come upon the principles of library system and legislation to their utmost perfection. The government is totally aware of the importance of its duty to disseminate knowledge to the people and it declares that fact. It consciously creates a storehouse of recorded knowledge for the benefit of the people. Our modern governments are yet to reach these levels.

Pliny in his natural history describes the public library planned by Julius Caesar and established by his friend Asinias Pollo in 39 BC. Pliny tells us that Asinias Polo had made men's talents and mental powers a public possession[5]. The principle that ''library should be for all'' was very dominant during those times. In Alexandria Ptolemies established in Third century BC a library with magnificent collection of 7,00,000 volumes[6]. This library was headed by many great scholars like Aristophanes and Callimachus. Callimachus devised a catalogue with author, title and subject entries. This library allowed free access to the people. At Pergmum another library with two lakhs volumes existed which Antony gifted to Cleopatra. In Rome the idea of a public library with large collection of volumes designed for common use first found practical realization in the time of first Roman Emperor Augustus who ruled between 63 BC to 14 AD.

Ancient Indian Libraries

India also has got a very ancient history of library systems, techniques and laws. Right from days of antiquity, Indian culture, philosophy and religion occupied a place of pride throughout the world and the neighbouring countries were all under the magic spell of its splendour and magnificence. Thousands of scholars from all over the world took hazardous journeys to use the huge collections of our recorded knowledge arranged in the most helpful sequence in our ancient seats of learning[7]. They were open to all irrespective of caste, creed or religion for any length of time. Even free boarding and lodging facilities were given to the needy users from far away places, for the period during which they used the collection. Even though they were known as academic libraries; those at Nalanda, Taxila and Pataliputra showed more free public library character than any of the present day libraries of that size[8].

Education in Ancient Kerala

Kerala, the secluded southern corner of India also has got a library history parallel to that of India. The beginning of educational and cultural activity in Kerala may also be traced back to very ancient times. In ancient period Kerala as an integral part of the socio-cultural unit called Tamilakam formed part of the educational system of Tamils. As in other parts of India in Tamilakam also religion influenced all aspects of life, especially education. Theology laid down the law and the rules of conduct. Among them was the faith that free gift to knowledge and its carrier-books as charity would earn merit for the giver and that this merit could be exchanged beneficially in the life after death. For example according to Manu the ancient codifier of law in India, free book service would earn even more of merit than the gift of the whole earth. Thus religion was one generator of force leading to free book service in those ancient days[9].

When we search through the sources for study of education and library system in ancient Kerala, in the Sangam works composed during the first four centuries of AD we come upon instances which reveal to us that collections of recorded information formed an integral part of the education in Kerala from very ancient days. The places where collections of manuscripts were maintained were considered as important centres of learning and most significant place of education and wisdom. There is an ancient Sanskrit saying which means that to have a library is to be an educator. This gives us an idea of the prestige, privilege and responsibility of one who possessed a library.

Many stanzas of the Sangam work Purananuru tells us that in those days common people were very much aware of the importance of education and collections of manuscripts. Stanza 312 of Purananuru a classic of Sangam period states that it is the duty of father to educate his son so that he will become virtuous. Education was also not considered a too formal process limited within any age group or other boundaries. Avvaiar the most revered Sangam saint poetess advises to the young: ''learn while young; letter and number, claim esteem; avoid ignorance, covet to be versed in knowledge; learn all sciences and cease not to learn.'' During those days there were facilities to proceed studies on any division of knowledge uniformly by any one who has interest.

Scholar Home Public Libraries

The nature of the ancient libraries of Kerala were highly related to the education system of the people. The teaching learning method followed in ancient Kerala was the same practised in Gurukula System of education throughout India at that time. In ancient literature of South India there are copious references to teachers who would arrange for the teaching and maintenance of boarding and lodging of students. The great scholars moulded their family situations in a way in which it would blend with teaching learning process which they are to undertake. This resulted in hereditary specialization by families in specific subject fields. There were families in Kerala which specialized in particular subjects like Thaikkatt Illam in Architecture[10]. In Ayurveda, Indian system of medicine there were eight great families, hereditary custodians of the science and practice of medicine well known throughout India[11]. In martial arts, in astrology, even in literature we can find families maintaining such tradition. These houses can be compared to the subject departments of the present day universities or specialized research institutions. Access to them was more free than the present days. Qualification was purely merit and devotion. But inside, life and work was more strict and tough than we people can imagine in our present day situations. It goes without saying that these scholar houses possessed great wealth of manuscripts on their topic of interest for the use of teachers, students and the interested users who came searching for them. Many original works and commentaries were written there. Each of the generations added their contribution to these collections. These collections of knowledge were undoubtedly neatly classified and catalogued and preserved in the best possible manner with reverence by persons who have familiarity with the thought content of these documents. Still Kerala maintains this tradition in some subject fields such as martial arts, music, Ayurveda, dance etc. and at these ancient houses we can still see huge collections of valuable manuscripts on their subjects preserved with utmost care for use.

This was the library situation of ancient Kerala after manuscripts and other ancient forms of books became popular. They are to be considered as public libraries, for they were open to all. The only difference they had with the institutions which we call public libraries was their specialization which gives an academic library character. But their services were available to all seekers and not limited to students. More than that different collections of various subjects that existed in a region, formed together a network without itself being aware of it. In their totality they formed a system almost like our public library system. Specialization of units gave them efficiency.

Library Services by Government

The South was also familiar with huge recorded collections as in Assyria and Alexandria. There is a tradition about a big library established by the king functioning at Madura in the Sangam age two thousand years ago[12]. It would not have suddenly come into or went out of existence. There would have been in existence such huge libraries for long time at many places in South India.

Gradually temples and Government entered into the field of education and organization and dissemination of knowledge. Temples became centres of all cultural activities and naturally educational institutions formed part of the temple establishments. When the great centres of advanced learning and their libraries at Nalanda, Vallabhi, Vikramasila etc. existed in North, institutions similar to them existed in Kerala. They are commonly called *salas* or *chalas.* Usually they were attached to temples. Most important of them were Kandaloor Salai, Parthivasekarapuram Salai, Sreevallabapuram Salai, Tiruvalla

Salai, Tirunelli Salai and Kottarakkara Salai[13]. Most of them were very much like Post-Graduate Institutions which imparted higher education in special subjects[14]. All expenses of education including food and accommodation were met by temples. Kandaloor Salai was an ancient institution; the Nalanda of the South and it was looked upon as a model by the people of that time. In Kandaloor Salai even a martial art department was there. It gave training to young who opted for military service. This subjugated the Salai to incessant attacks by Cholas, the enemy kingdom, and caused its destruction. There were all facilities for students to get instruction in any subject and proceed by themselves in the higher branches of knowledge. Their collections of manuscripts were vast and varied. The organization and service was efficient. These centres of learning played important part in propagating knowledge and culture and all these institutions had their libraries which contained books in all branches of learning which were being copied from time to time[15].

Professional Status of Libraries

Librarianship was also considered an esteemed profession in ancient Kerala. During the period of the scholar home libraries, and Salais only highly educated persons could work as librarians. The person who kept the documents had to have a very good knowledge about the thought contents of the documents. This tradition of scholar librarians continued upto the medieval period. The copper plate grant of king Trailokyamalla, a Chalukyan ruler, 1058 AD furnishes details of an educational institution maintained by him. It was equipped with a library with six Saraswathi Bhandarikas (librarians). The inscription further furnishes us details regarding distribution of land which tells us the dignified and honoured position; the librarians had in temple colleges and other cultural and educational institutions; "35 matter of land under the dam Aratura and Diggavige at Nagavaer to the expounder of Butadarsana, 30 matter of land to the expounder of Nyaya, 45 matter of land to the expounder of Prabakara and 30 matter to each Saraswathi Bhandarikas."

The importance which the ancient people gave to the collection and dissemination of recorded knowledge; the role they assigned to the library in educational process contributed to the academic excellence of those times, fruits of which are the ancient classics which comes to us from those times. Kural the classified and neatly arranged little work said to be a mustard seed containing the whole universe of knowledge, Purattirattu a book of about 2000 abstracts of all the important works of the South India and many other works which in their way of referencing, footnotes etc. outshines present day research works took birth at that time due to the merit of the information support system[16]. In modern times such works rarely occur. Any qualitative assessment of contributions to knowledge done during the ancient days, in comparison with the present will reveal that our ancestors were in a higher level than us.

The hundred years war between the Cheras and the Pandyas destroyed most of the educational institutions and libraries. Then Aryans who started migrating into Kerala from eighth century slowly gained upper hand in Kerala society. Result was introduction of caste system and loss of access to educational institutions for some classes. The next centuries in which major kingdoms of Kerala took their shape, were full of wars between kings to establish their authorities and mark their boundaries. All that was remaining of the traditional schools, libraries etc. also got disturbed and disappeared. Before the rulers settled for their socio-political and administrative reforms; came the foreign intervention with the landing of Vasco Da Gama. As a result of all these confusion and the diversion of interest, rulers and people turned away from educational and cultural spheres of life. More and more people became illiterate[17].

Free Access to All

Almost all works on history of public libraries considers it an institution of recent origin; that of the nineteenth century. So there are many arguments against considering these ancient libraries as public libraries. Mostly ancient libraries existed as part of academic institutions and so we usually classify them under academic libraries. But as we have seen in Kerala's ancient days those libraries were freely open to all and were able to give authentic and efficient information service to the public than our present day public libraries. In our present day also distance education, which only can reach 75 per cent of the common people who cannot approach formal system, is using public libraries as their study centres. So in all times libraries will inevitably be connected with education. Another argument that ancient libraries were mere storehouses also cannot stand. The fruits of their activity are still lively present in our culture. Then the collections were private, were also not a matter of concern, for as we saw in Kerala's scholar homes they are maintained for the people.

Even in these days of mushroom growth of new institutions, it is the principles of access—as Unesco defined; open for free and equal use of all members of society—is that which differentiates public library from other libraries. The popular view about the ancient libraries is that they were not accessible to the common people in general. They did not have therefore any direct link with and impact upon lives of the people. But, the study of ancient Kerala's libraries shows that the view is not true. In ancient Kerala education as well as access to houses of recorded knowledge was open to all and there was a high level of literacy[18]. Acquiring knowledge was not a privilege confined to any class or caste is proved by the fact that scholars of Sangam period were drawn from all walks of life and from all tribes of ancient south. According to an estimate; among the 192 Sangam poets, there were 13 kings, 29 brahmins, 57 vellalas, 36 women, 17 hillmen, 13 foresters, 7 vaniyars, 7 artisans, 1 shepherd, 1 potter etc.[19] Paranar and Kapilar the great Sangam poets of Kerala, and Avvayar belonged to the Pana caste which is a lower caste in present society. If we consider the present day; 90 per cent of the scholars will be from upper strata of society. In ancient days it was not like that. Even female education was not neglected. As a result we hear several scholarly women who contributed much to the cultural life of their times. Purananuru mentions about 15 poetesses by name, most of them belonging to castes now considered inferior[20]. So in ancient Kerala education was more democratic and all the record collections maintained by educational institutions were maintained for the whole society.

Origins of Library Legislation

But like the arguments on limitations in use put against the view of free access to all, to some extent restrictions were there in the access to these ancient collections and their use. An inscription of Kerala king Karunandakan (857-890 AD) tells us the existence of strict rules inside the Salai's of Kerala[21]. But even in these days we cannot find any library which is open to us without any rules and restrictions. Without some prescribed rules and procedures; no institution can exist. In ancient days these restrictions were more severe. But they were meant to protect those manuscripts and their information from destruction. Books in the modern sense were unknown and all that those libraries possessed were manuscripts copied with infinite care and patient labour and often at considerable expense. Most of them existed in originals only and if they are lost or destroyed the knowledge stored is also lost for ever to the society. So rules for their preservation and restrictions on their use were strictly enforced; but judiciously. They were made available to all those real seekers of that particular thought content. In these ancient customs and rules created and adhered to maximise the utility of those graphic records to society; we find the primitive stages of library legislation. Common customary law and laws and decrees passed by kings to promote the welfare of the greatest numbers; are all legislation in its broad outlook.

Eventhough the terms 'library' or 'public library' was not in existence, the social institution which gathered, preserved and disseminated knowledge existed in Kerala along with the communicating man. They reached their most active period when the scholar homes and Salais existed in Kerala. When we evaluate them giving consideration of the limitations of those times and in comparison with the present state of public libraries in Kerala which we consider progressive, we find that the organisation and service of those ancient days were more specialized, efficient, reliable and authentic. They suited the society that created them than the present setup suiting the present day society. Even then as said by Thompson, it is too strange to have to argue that library systems, their basic rules and principles have by and large been established over a very long period of time.

REFERENCES

1. Thompson, James. *History of Principles of Librarianship.* London: Clive Bingley, 1977.
2. Hessel, Alfred. *A History of Libraries.* Translated by Reuben Peiss. Washington: Scare Crow, 1977.
3. Dunlap, Leslie W. *Readings in Library History.* London: RR Bowker, 1972.
4. Thompson. *Op. cit.,* 1.
5. *Ibid.*
6. Olle, James G. *Library History.* London: Clive Bingley, 1967.
7. Raman Nair, R. National Library: A historical perspective. *International Library Movement,* 1987, Vol.9, No.1.
8. *Ibid.*
9. Ranganathan, S.R. Free book service for all: *An International Survey.* Bombay: Asia, 1968.
10. Nilakanta Sastri, K.A. *History of South India from Prehistoric Times to Present.* London: OUP, 1959.
11. *Ibid.*

12. Gopinath, M.A. Madras. In Ranganathan *Op. cit.*, 9.
13. Kunjan Pillai, Elamkulam P.N. *Studies in Kerala History*. Kottayam: NBS, 1970.
14. Ramachandran Nair, Adoor K.K. Kerala state gazetter, Trivandrum: *State Gazetters,* 1986, Vol. 2, Part 1.
15. Nilakanta Sastri. *Op. cit.,* 10.
16. Raman Nair, R. *Public Library Systems in Ancient South India.* ILA Bulletin, Vol. 12, No. 3, 1991.
17. Sreedhara Menon, Ed. *Kerala District Gazetteers:* Trivandrum. Trivandrum: Govt. Press, 1962.
18. Kunjan Pillai, *Op. cit.,* 13.
19. Ramachandran Nair. *Op. cit.,* 14.
20. *Ibid.*
21. Gopinatha Rao, Ed. *Travancore Archeological Series.* Vol.1, Trivandrum: Government Press, 1947.

4

IDENTIFICATION AND AWARENESS

The term public library was commonly used from the beginning of nineteenth century to denote the institutions which store and disseminate information in society. The wide popularity and growth in numbers of such institutions were also the features that they acquired at the beginning of nineteenth century. Various social and cultural forces directly and indirectly contributed to the establishment of a large number of public libraries and their development in Kerala at the beginning of nineteenth century.

It was the alarming increase of illiteracy that led to the intervention of the State in the sphere of education and the formulation of a positive educational policy. In Kerala the direct activity of the State in the field of education began when Her Highness Rani Gouri Parvathi Bai, with the assistance of Col. Munro introduced a system of free and compulsory education under State control in 1817 AD[1]. Maharaja Swathi Tirunal (1829-1847) a versatile genius and great man of high accomplishments continued these educational reforms. He is considered to be the ruler of Kerala who laid the foundation of modern system of education in Kerala. In 1830's English education was recognized as a civilizing agency and government started patronising the spread of English education by opening English schools. It was he who started in 1836 the first English public school in Travancore[2]. District schools were also started in the same year.

Trivandrum Public Library, 1829

At the beginning of nineteenth century, in Kerala also there was no institution with the name public library. The first public library and the oldest of its kind in India came into existence during Swathi Tirunal's reign. The then British resident of Travancore was Col. Edward Cadogan. Cadogan was the grandson of Sir Hans Sloans, the founder of the British Museum and he could very easily make the Maharaja and high officials aware of the need and importance of libraries in a modern educational system. Swathy Tirunal was also a great scholar in many languages, a poet, a musician, and a musical composer of very high order. He was easily impressed by the idea of an institution like British Museum. Joining together they established in 1829 the Trivandrum Public Library[3]. The king took active interest in the affairs of that public library throughout his reign. The library was first managed by an association called Trivandrum Public Library Committee of which the British Resident was the President. In 1889 the Trivandrum Public Library Committee entered into an agreement with the Government according to which their entire assets were handed over to the Government[4]. The condition was that the Government would erect a suitable building for a new library for the benefit of the public and to that end provide a well stocked furnished reference library and should undertake the maintenance of the samc in a suitable manner under such regulations as may be best calculated to carry out the end in view. Accordingly Government took over the management of Trivandrum Public Library and it was treated as one of the minor departments of the State[5]. The British Resident continued to serve as the president of the committee.

Education and Libraries in Cochin

In Cochin, the Government undertook the responsibility of educating the people in 1818 when the first state owned schools were started there[6]. District schools were started in 1877. Christian Missionaries also established many educational institutions in different parts of Travancore, Cochin and Malabar area. In the later half of the nineteenth century Governments of Travancore and Cochin began to patronise English education at higher levels and so opened a lot of English schools and colleges. The first college was started in 1875. In all these educational institutions very efficient library services were also organized on the pattern of library service available in Britain. The teachers and library staff were usually Britishers at the beginning. The products of these educational institutions realized the value of libraries. They took initiative in influencing the rulers to establish libraries in different parts of the country; so that libraries will be accessible to them in their public life also.

Government-supported public libraries were established at Ernakulam in 1869, Trichur in 1873, Kottayam in 1881, Tellichery in 1901, Calicut in 1924 and Cannanore in 1927[7]. These libraries continuously maintained good collections and services up to 1950's.

Library Awareness

Social and political activists who used the services of libraries established by Government became aware of the wide possibilities of such institutions. Spread of education and the birth of a large number of newspapers and journals in the State and the revolutions that were going on in the social and political spheres of life kindled in the people a desire to have such public libraries very near to them so that they can also get the daily news and discuss on them. All these contributed to the birth of a people's library movement in the end of the nineteenth century, which we have to discuss as the next phases.

Government supported and nourished the people's movement. But at the same time Government continued its own independent projects of library development resulting in two parallel movements in the region's library field. Government's contributions strictly adhered to some generally accepted library principles which were static throughout next three phases. It is very much like an extension of second phase through later phases and so we have to discuss those developments here itself to avoid confusion.

Initiation of Modern Library Legislation

State Government was continuously active in library affairs. It was aware of its responsibility to establish and maintain library and information services for the people. During the reign of Sri Moolam Tirunal Maharaja of Travancore rules were framed to give grant-in-aid to libraries for the first time. The rules were published in Travancore Gazette in 1918. The conditions prescribed by this rule for a library to be eligible for grant are[8]:

* The libraries should be under the administrative control of a committee or officials recognized or appointed by the Director of Education.
* The reading facilities in the library must be open to all free of cost.

* No restrictions based on caste or religion should be imposed on its users.
* The rules of the library or reading room should be approved by the Director of Education.
* The accounts, registers and records should be maintained in a proper way and must be supplied for verification to the Assistant Inspector of Elementary Schools whenever he calls for them.

The rules also prescribed some minimum standards related to the collection to be maintained, services to be done etc. and explained the procedures for fixing the rate of annual grants, and grants for construction of building, and purchase of furnitures and equipments. It also sanctioned the issue of government publications free of cost or at reduced rates to these libraries.

These rules framed by the Government in its own initiative contain the basic objectives of public library and the most important factors of modern library legislation. In these rules Government accepted that libraries are also educational institutions which have to play a role equal to that of schools and colleges, in education. The rules accepts that it was Government's responsibility to establish and maintain library service for the public. The unique feature of the rules was its acceptance that public library service must be a free service to the public. The reading and consultation facilities are to be made available to the public free of cost by all the libraries that get Government grant. It was only from the later half of the nineteenth century that social forces worked towards free book service for all; even in western countries[9]. Providing totally free library service to the public is yet an ideal to be realized even in the States which have enacted legislation including the present day Kerala where this law was in force in those old days. Free supply of Government publications to libraries was also a progressive move provided in these rules.

Libraries for the Spread of Education

Government took, the encouragement of libraries as a part of its programme for expansion of educational facilities in the State. Before 1928 Government has established a number of libraries especially for the use of women[10]. The Travancore Educational Reform Committee under the Chairmanship of R.M. Statham, in 1932 made certain recommendations regarding the development of public libraries in order to advance education and to provide facilities for adult education. Immediate action followed. The Director of Public Instruction was asked to prepare a scheme and accordingly he prepared a scheme for establishment of a central circulating library and a large number of rural libraries. In 1935 the Government sanctioned the opening of sixty such rural libraries attached to departmental primary schools in important underdeveloped areas of the State. Government feared that literate people will lapse into illiteracy unless reading and study can be practised with the aid of libraries in these regions. Provision was made for each library to receive a particular number of periodicals and newspapers. The system gradually developed into 354 libraries with an average of 500 selected standard books and 42 newspapers and periodicals.

In Cochin also parallel development was going on during this period. The Government of Cochin began to establish experimental village libraries since 1926 in various parts of the State to support its programme of adult education[11]. In 1946 there were three types of libraries. Seventeen public libraries five major rural libraries and above five hundred village libraries. The annual expenditure for library development in the State during 1947-48 was Rs.50,000.

State Central Library

The Trivandrum Public Library run directly by the government from 1888 was transferred to the control of the University of Travancore in 1938[12]. A new committee was constituted by Government with Pro-Vice-Chancellor as the president and the University Librarian as secretary. The committee had full powers to manage the affairs of the institution and to approve all expenditure. But this transfer of institution met with resentments and protests from the library conscious public, and newspapers published editorials and a number of articles against this order. The apprehension was that, following the transfer of the library to the control of the university, the library may not be accessible to the public as before and the usefulness of the rich collection might be reduced, restricted and limited. The concern of the public expressed through newspapers and in some cultural functions during this period vindicated one thing. In the preceding half century during which it was a direct department of government, the library has served the public very efficiently. The discontinuation or change in its service was too disheartening to the literate public.

Due to this forceful public opinion, a resolution was unanimously passed by the legislature in 1948. It resolved that Government should take over the institution from the university and manage it as a separate department as was done up to 1938[13]. Accordingly the Government resumed the control of the institution in 1949. The committee was also reconstituted with the Minister for Education as President and the Librarian as the convenor of the committee. The committee continued to be in charge of the management of the library. In 1956 Government included this library in the plan scheme and sanctioned about seven lakhs rupees for converting the library into State Central Library and the District Distributing Library for Trivandrum. A State Librarian was also appointed. To increase the library's usefulness and to extend its services half a dozen libraries from the northern border to the southern border of the State were affiliated to it within two years.

Local Library Authorities

Malabar region which formed part of the Madras State and which came to Kerala with the re-organization of States had in 1956 about 500 libraries excluding those run by Local Library Authority under the provisions of Madras Library Act. Local Library Authority was constituted in 1951 for the whole of Malabar. The Calicut Municipal Library with a large collection of books was converted into District Central Library under the local authority. The Government later divided Malabar into revenue districts namely Calicut, Cannanore and Palghat. So three Local Library Authorities started functioning in 1959 according to the provisions of Madras Public Library Act. Recently Kasaragad and Malappuram Districts were formed dividing Cannanore and Calicut. In each district, local library authority has a district central library at district headquarters and branch libraries under it.

Rules and Standards

In 1959 Government issued an order constituting a State Library Advisory Board[14]. The Board consisted fifteen members with Minister for Education as Chairman, Director of Public Instruction as Secretary and State Librarian ex-officio member. The functions of the Board were to formulate rules related to libraries and advise the Government on the affairs of the libraries and the Kerala Granthasala Sangham. Through an order issued in 1958 the Government channelized the disbursement of grants to rural libraries through District Education

Officers[15]. Another order concerning the grant for construction of library buildings and purchase of equipments made the libraries strictly adhere to the approved designs published with that order, for building and equipments[16]. In 1966 government decided to continue a system of grant-in-aid to libraries until a Library Act could be passed. The various rules and orders relating to the payment of grant to libraries were consolidated by a Government Order[17]. This order made provisions for; annual grant to libraries, building and furnitures grant to libraries, annual grant to Granthasala Sangham and allowances to librarians. In 1971 Government constituted a gradation committee which is to tour throughout the State and review and report about the libraries receiving grant[18]. In 1976 and 1981 government issued orders classifying the libraries into six grades and fixing the different rates of their annual grants[19].

Such a long, continuous and live involvement of State in library affairs is a rare phenomena. The concept followed by the State in library development was establishing and maintaining public libraries in all places as independent self sufficient units. State also fully supported people's move for establishing and maintaining such units almost independent of State control. When the modern concept of each public library as service outlet of a library and information dissemination system for the people took birth State tried to establish such a system. But interests of other groups involved in this activity clashed with the new ideals and delayed State's Act. Evenwhile trying unsuccessfully for this modernization, State continued the development according to the earlier concept and maintained its existing library service in tact and continued the developments in accordance with earlier methods.

REFERENCES

1. Velu Pillai, T.K. *Travancore state manual.* Trivandrum: Government Press, 1947.
2. Sreedhara Menon, Ed. *Kerala district gazetteers:* Trivandrum. Trivandrum: Government Press, 1962.
3. Trivandrum Public Library. Administration report. Trivandrum: Government Press, 1981.
4. Sreedhara Menon. *Op. cit.,* 2.
5. Raman Nair, R. Public library development in Kerala: a historical perspective. Proceedings of South Indian History Congress. Dharwad, Karnataka University, 1992.
6. Achutha Menon. Cochi Rajyacharitham. Calicut: *Mathrubhoomi,* 1989.
7. Kerala, Legislature, Secretariat of -. Kerala Public Library Bill 1971: Background materials. Trivandrum: The Author, 1972.

8. Travancore Gazette No.39, Education sheet, 9th Kanni 1093 M.E. (1918 AD) Trivandrum: Government Press.
9. Ranganathan, S.R. *Free Book Service for All: An International Survey.* Bombay: Asia, 1968.
10. Panikkar, P.N. Ed. *Keralathile Granthasala Prasthanam.* Trivandrum. Steps, 1982.
11. Kerala, Legislature, *Op. cit.,* 7.
12. Sreedhara Menon. *Op. cit.,* 2.
13. *Ibid.*
14. Panikkar. *Op. cit.,* 10.
15. Travancore-Cochin. Government Order No. M 98 dtd. 5.2.1958.
16. Kerala. Government Order. MS No. 429. Edn: dtd. 25.7.1961.
17. Kerala. Government Order. RL No. 843/66/Edn. dtd. 30.3.1966.
18. Kerala. Government Order. RJ No.1186 Edn. dtd. 4.8.1971.
19. Kerala. Government Order. RJ No. 375/76/H Edn. dtd. 21.2.1976 and MS No. 39/81/H Edn. dtd. 9.3.1989.

5

MOVEMENT OF THE PEOPLE

In Kerala, the Government has contributed much to the growth and modernization of libraries than anywhere else in India continuously throughout nineteenth and twentieth centuries. But in library field, Kerala is known not for the library activities of the State but for a century old people's library movement. It was a unique movement in its nature and growth. It has a spontaneous growth from the minds of the people. It grew parallel to the library development projects of the State.

Various social and political forces directly or indirectly contributed to the birth and growth of people's library movement. The second half of the nineteenth century witnessed the full flowering of national political consciousness and the growth of an organized national movement in India[1]. This resulted in recognizing the increased importance of the individual. Creating public opinion and spreading political ideas waranted an educated and informed public. Political workers therefore gave more emphasis to social education activities including the establishment of public libraries. The people's library movement got special impetus, also from the emergence of political parties, social reform movements, communal and religious organizations and the struggle for responsible government in the State[2].

Political and Social Reformation

The spread of western education influenced movements for social and political reform in Kerala from the end of nineteenth century. Rulers of Kerala were benevolent and modern in outlook. So most of the people's movements were bloodless revolutions that reaped victory. The first legislature in any Indian State was set up by the Maharaja of Travancore in 1888[3]. Three years later representatives of the slowly growing middle class presented to the king a memorial known as Malayale Momorial, signed by more than 10,000 persons. It appealed to the king to give a share to the people in the administration of the State which was then largely done by persons imported from Madras. This agitation continued for a decade. It awakened the middle class of Travancore to a sense of their inherent rights, thereby paving the way for a new chapter in the political history of the State[4].

In all the communities in Kerala, from the highest to the lowest in social strata; obsolete customs and practices were alive during nineteenth century. The western educated and progressive minded younger generation started reform activities and resisted outdated customs, traditions and systems of inheritance, succession and family organization.

National Movement

Freedom movement also developed the spirit of library movement in Kerala. In 1903 Indian National Congress held a large public meeting at Calicut under the Chairmanship of a veteren Congress leader C. Vijaya Raghavacharyar[5]. In 1910 a branch of the famous Home Rule League of Mrs. Annie Besant was formed in Malabar[6]. Civil Disobedience Movement of 1930 and 1932-33 and regional social movements like Guruvayoor Temple Satyagraha for permitting the lower caste people to enter into the temple stirred the Kerala society, peasants, workers, teachers and many other groups became organized and were drawn into politics[7]. In the forties besides Quit India Movement the agitation for self-government in Travancore and Cochin States gathered momentum. In Travancore the Travancore State Congress and in Cochin the Cochin Prajamandalam led the movement. The common culture, language, literature and the parallel social and political reform movements going on in the States of Kerala, Cochin and Malabar and the spread of national movement quickly gave birth to the idea of a United Kerala by the dissolution of the political boundaries which kept them as distinct political units[8].

The newspaper that is having even today the largest circulation in Kerala, *Malayala Manorama* came into existence in 1890 followed by numerous dailies and periodicals. Swadeshabhimani K. Ramakrishna Pillai edited the papers *Darpanam, Kerala Panchika,* Malayali and *Swadeshabhimani* between 1899 and 1910. Copies of these dailies reached every village library. The articles he wrote under the pseudonym

Keralan were highly critical of the administration. He came to be hailed everywere as a stout champion of popular liberties. *Kerala Kaumudhi* was started in 1911 and *Mathrubhoomi* which contributed much to the spread of national movement and the paper in which many who actively participated in the freedom struggle also associated; started its publication in 1923. In 1924 another newspaper named *Al-amin* was also started from Calicut under the editorship of Mohammed Abdur Rahman with the object of bringing Muslims into the stream of national movement. Numerous dailies and periodicals were started by different political, religious and communal organizations to support their activities. Newspapers carried details of the political and social reform activities that are going on around. It was the only medium of communication available in those days and people anxiously waited for every issue. In 1910 when Swadeshbhimani K. Ramakrishna Pillai, the pioneer of fearless journalism who was waging a crusade against the administration of the then Dewan was arrested and deported it had its repercussions all over Kerala[9].

Seeds of People's Library Movement

It was the newspapers and the curiosity for the daily news that prompted the speedy establishment of thousands of village libraries in a very short period. Because all people cannot afford a daily newspaper, at every house where a paper was subscribed people of nearby houses assembled. Sri. P.N. Panikkar the leading figure of people's library movement in Kerala, and the most noted activist over half a century remembers the starting of one such library named Sanathana Dharma Vayanasala[10]: "Only a few important wealthy persons could subscribe to newspapers in villages. Due to my thirst to know about the social and political movements that were blowing around, I somehow managed to subscribe a newspaper at my house. It was *Sreevashumkodu National Daily*. Five to eight persons assembled everyday at my house and they asked me to read the paper aloud. I felt happy about it. I also used to read to them biographies of Great men in days when we missed the paper. Sri. P.N. Madhavan Pillai a friend of mine subscribed two other dailies and he had a small collection of books. Pooling together these books and newspapers in a small room freely rented out for the purpose; we started the small library". Like this, houses in many of the villages of Kerala became places of reading and discussion, and were the seeds of the people's library movement. People donated their personal collections and also subscribed newspapers and periodicals for these libraries. Educated youngsters from the villages offered their voluntary service to organise and manage these village libraries and reading rooms.

Nationalist Writings

Writings of Mahatma Gandhi and other leaders of the national movement exercised tremendous influence on the people. The persons who undertook leadership in social and political reform movements in Kerala read and translated those works into regional language.

In Kerala during the days of the national movement, the persons belonging to the Congress Socialist Party which developed within the Congress took active interest in cultural renaissance. They knew that political and literary works dramas and discussions were the best mediums used throughout the world to educate the public, to rouse their political and social consciousness and to kindle the fire of revolutions[11]. Result was a progressive literature movement. A flood of novels, dramas and poems dealing with social political and economic issues appeared. They were produced with the intention of creating an awareness of their rights among the peasants workers and lower middle class and to infuse into them the thought of the need to fight for their rights.

But majority of people remained beyond the reach of these mediums due to illiteracy, poverty and lack of communication systems. So the political and social reformers searched for venues closest to the people from where almost a natural dialogue with the common people can become possible. Their search ended in the venues or institutions that were public libraries. Many public libraries like Trivandrum Public Library established by Government were functioning satisfactorily, disseminating knowledge, news and ideas to the people. Already many libraries on this model were established by the people with their own initiative. The first attempt by the people to establish such an institution was during the reign of Visakam Tirunal Maharaja. With his support a library named Suguna Poshini was established in 1880 at Vanchiyoor Trivandrum and a vast collection of Malayalam books was organized there[12]. The SRMV Association Library at Karamana started functioning in 1888. Jnanapradayini Library of Neyyattinkara, Sankara Vilasam Library of Chengannoor and Chithira Tirunal Smaraka Granthasala of Trivandrum came into existence before 1920 due to people's initiative[13].

All these libraries conducted literary and cultural activities and discussions on topics of current interest. The contributions of Chithira Tirunal Smaraka Granthasala of Vanchiyoor to Kerala culture and literature was enormous. For almost six decades it functioned in close association with the most notable cultural and literary figures. Popularisation of standard literature and arts done by this institution was to a remarkable extent.

Venues to Spread Reform Movements

The political and social activists found in these libraries their base, the nucleus in society from where they can spread their reform movements and activities. With this motive they involved or infiltrated in the existing people's libraries. They used them and also established thousands of new libraries in the places where they were not already available. The Congress and Communist workers organized in them study circles, evening classes, adult education programmes etc. The novels, poems and essays of the progressive literary movement were usually circulated through these libraries. Their dramas which discussed the social, political and economic problems; produced with the intention of attracting and retaining more workers for the national movement and for forming public opinion were staged in connection with the programmes organized by these libraries. Enormous quantity of reading materials discussing the political and social problems, published by the political parties, communal organizations, trade unions, youth associations, women's organizations etc. flowed into these village libraries. The increased use of the libraries and reading rooms have raised them to the level of cultural centres of the localities. This tendency was more noticeable in the rural areas and therefore apparently the villages were the beneficiaries. In fact these libraries and reading rooms attained almost the position occupied by temples in medieval Kerala[14]. They were similar to the scholar homes and Salais we came upon in the ancient Kerala in few aspects. The depth of the knowledge activity, the ancient institutions have had the new ones lacked. But the inviting atmosphere was present here also.

REFERENCES

1. Bipin Chandra. *Modern India.* New Delhi: NCERT, 1971.
2. Raman Nair, R. Origins of people's library movement in Kerala. *Granthana,* Vol.

7, No.1, 1994

3. Ramakrishnan Nair. *Constitutional Experiments in Kerala.* Trivandrum: The Author, 1964.
4. Sreedhara Menon, A. *A Survey of Kerala History.* Kottayam: SPCS, 1976.
5. Damodaran, K. and Narayana Pillai, C. *Keralathile Swatantriya Samaram.* Trivandrum: KBS, 1958.
6. *Ibid.*
7. *Ibid.*
8. Raman Nair, R. Role of village libraries in social and political reform in Kerala. In *LIS: Some Perspectives.* S. Panduranga Reddy Fescrift Volume. Hyderabad, SPFVC, 1998
9. *Ibid.*
10. Panikkar, P.N., Ed. *Keralathile Granthasala Prasthanam.* Trivandrum: Steps, 1987.
11. Parameshwaran Nair. *Malayala Sahitya Charitram.* Kottayam: SPCS, 1973.
12. Sreedhara Menon, Ed. *Kerala District Gazetteers: Trivandrum.* Trivandrum: Government Press, 1962.
13. Ramanujan Nair, R. *Library Movement in Kerala.* Trivandrum: Writers Club, 1974.
14. Namboodiripad, E.M.S. *Keralam Malayalikalude Mathrubhoomi.* Trivandrum: Chinta, 1969.

6

SOCIO-CULTURAL FORCE

During the first-half of the nineteenth century village libraries grew up throughout the length and breadth of Kerala like mushrooms. The wide political and social activities of the time aroused curiosity of the people for daily news. These village libraries were expected to support the desire of the common people to have a place in the community from where they can get the daily news. The non-specialized nature and non-serious base work assigned to them were the causes for this instantaneous birth. Like mushrooms most of them were short lived ones. Hundreds of libraries took birth every year while hundreds of them also died. Most of the libraries were established as a result of the initial enthusiasm of some local political or social activists. Loss of interest of such persons or groups which established the libraries and political rivalries or clash of individual interests caused their death.

Attempts to Organize Library Movement

The emergence of such large number of libraries in the villages and small towns of Kerala, the difficulties experienced in running them and the breakdown and collapse of several of them forced the attention of some serious library workers to the need for a library movement. In 1925 for the first time the activists of the people's library movement and some important persons from various spheres of activity in Kerala assembled together to exchange ideas and discuss the problems and possibilities for sustaining the village libraries. Under the auspices of; Jnanapradayini Library at Neyyattinkara in 1925, Sree Chithira Tirunal Library at Trivandrum in 1933 and Diwan Nanu Pillai Memorial Library at Neyyoor in 1937, three All Travancore Library Conferences were held[1]. Academicians and leading literary and legal luminaries of

Travancore like Prof. C.V. Chandrasekaran, P.K. Narayana Pillai and Malloor Govinda Pillai participated in those conferences. These conferences succeeded in making the public feel the need of a library movement. It also brought the attention of the Government to its responsibility in aiding and assisting libraries.

In Cochin State also the people became aware of the need for an organized library movement during the end of 1920's. Many library activists from Cochin area, prominent persons who later became political leaders and administrators like Ambat Sivarama Menon,–later Chief Minister of Cochin, attended the fourth All India Library Conference held in 1927 at Madras[2]. They hastened the library activities in Cochin. In 1931 "Samastha Kerala Pustakalaya Samithi"; an association of libraries was started in Trichur in Cochin State[3]. This association could not do much except publishing the first issue of a quarterly called *Grantha Viharam.*

Kerala Granthalaya Sangham, 1943

In June 1937, the first Malabar Library Conference was held at Calicut. K. Kelappan, the veteran freedom fighter was the Chairman of that Conference. It gave birth to the organization called 'Malabar Vayanasala Sangham'[4]. The office bearers were all active political leaders of the region. They could not devote adequate attention to library work, and hence library movement suffered. With the aim of revitalizing this organization and to extend its sphere of activity to the whole of Kerala a meeting was held in 1943 at Tellichery[5]. As per its resolution this organization was registered as Kerala Granthalaya Sangham in December 1943 and this was in theory the first all Kerala organization for the library movement. It did tremendous work until 1953 for the establishment and development of libraries in Malabar area[6]. On its invitation Dr. S.R. Ranganathan visited the libraries in Malabar area in 1945 and delivered lectures on various aspects of library development, for the library and social activists. After 1953 this association became inactive.

At this stage the library activists were between two crucial problems. Firstly they have to impress the public. The failure of all the earlier efforts to organize the library movement at the regional or State level, discouraged the general public and also most of the library workers from becoming more active for this purpose. People were satisfied with mere availability of newspapers and light reading materials. They are to be made aware that without a strong movement to support these small libraries they cannot exist. They have also to impress upon the Government that library services are vital to the mainstream of life and that libraries require more attention than taking it as a side business.

But this time library workers throughout the State became convinced that the numerous libraries in Kerala could not be sustained either or by the usual donation of the interested reading public or by nominal assistance by the government or by both. There must be adequate regular income for the library service. They also felt convinced that a central organization with dedicated workers and steady income is essential to maintain these libraries continuously functional and also prevent their winding up.

Kerala Granthasala Sangham, 1945

A meeting of the librarians at Ambalapuzha in North Travancore in August 1945 under the auspices of the well managed P.K. Memorial Library resolved to form a central organization to fill the gap. As a result the All Travancore Granthasala Sangham was formed with membership of 47 libraries represented at the meeting[7]. With the integration of the Travancore-Cochin State in 1949, name of the Sangham was changed to Travancore-Cochin Granthasala Sangham, and later when the Kerala State was formed in 1956, it assumed its present title Kerala Granthasala Sangham[8].

At the first meeting Sri. K.M. Kesavan was elected as President and Sri. P.N. Panikkar as Secretary of the Sangham[9]. From the first election in 1945 Sri. P.N. Panikkar was continuously elected President of the Sangham. With his dedicated work as the moving spirit Sangham has rendered an estimable service to the cultural renaissance of Kerala. It has become a movement which has no counterpart anywhere in the world.

In the beginning the functions which Sangham undertook were modest. It aimed to function as the central organization of all existing libraries in the State. The preliminary programmes prepared by the Sangham were[10]:

* To enroll all existing libraries as members.
* To revive and rejuvenate all defunct and stagnant libraries.
* To establish libraries in the regions where there are none.
* To strengthen the organization by enrolling more individual members.
* To connect common fund.

* To give publicity to the movement through the publication of pamphlets and booklets and by conducting public meetings with a view to canvass support.

Dewan Sir C.P. Ramaswamy Aiyer

For all its activities Sangham hoped to get encouragement and assistance from Government. When the Sangham started its activities the Dewan of Travancore was the able and illustrious administrator Sir C.P. Ramaswamy Aiyer. He was also a known scholar and a person who has widely travelled in Western countries. The activists of the Sangham decided to meet the Dewan for getting assistance to its working. To pursue the matter a committee with Sri P.N. Panikkar as Secretary was deputed. The delegation was received on 6th August 1946 by the Dewan of Travancore[11].

Dewan was very helpful and sympathetic towards the library movement. It was his encouragement and assistance that gave confidence and strength to the Sangham at its initial stage. Actually Dewan was opposed to the Travancore State Congress the pioneer political party championing the cause of self government. He was also against the national movement that was brewing in the State. He knew that the library activists are all from these movements. Even then he supported the library movement which nourished all these movements.

When the delegation met the Dewan in his office he very heartily welcomed them and gave a lecture to them on the contributions that public libraries have done in developed countries of the world. He encouraged them to proceed on[12]. The demand for increasing the allowance and a monthly grant for appointing organizers were sanctioned on the spot. The Dewan advised the delegates to register the Sangham under The Charitable and Educational Societies Act and after that approach him again for further increase in grants. Within a short time, the Dewan consulting with the officials sanctioned the other demands of the Sangham also. The services of Sri P.N. Panikkar and another activist Sri P. Madhavan Pillai was let to the Sangham. Instructions were issued to enroll libraries under Travancore University as members of the Sangham[13]. Even in these days no Government will be bold enough to connect academic library systems into the public library system for the benefit of the common people, the majority who cannot normally approach the higher educational institutions. Dewan's concept was more democratic than what we later practiced under democratic governments. The encouragement that these acts of Dewan gave to the people's library movement was enormous. He was really interested in establishing a good public library system in the State. Even while he was totally disturbed by a lot of political problems, he accepted the request to inaugurate the All Travancore Library Conference at Ambalapuzha on 13th October 1946 in which the Sangham's policies were framed. There he had given a very impressive talk on the need for a well organized library system in Travancore.

Activities of the Sangham

As soon as the Sangham obtained the services of organizers, it set-up the following minimum programmes for them to execute[14]. They have to:

* Enroll a minimum of four new libraries in a division every month;
* Establish at least one library or reading room every month;
* Organize one Taluk union a month and hold at least one meeting in every two months;
* Prepare and submit detailed survey report regarding libraries in a Taluk; Organize at least one adult education centre;
* Inspect member libraries in each Taluk and record the rate of progress;
* Organize public meetings in every Taluk with the view to propagate the values of library movement; and
* In accordance with the directions from the Sangham; to hold library conferences and library exhibition and re-organize libraries etc.

On 3rd February 1947, Sangham organized at Kottayam that year's All Travancore Library Conference. It advanced the objectives and programmes of the Sangham which were already framed. The conference requested the government to organize a library department. Eventhough the conference considered the draft of the library development plan and Library Bill for Travancore sent to the Dewan by Dr. S.R. Ranganathan the leaders of the Sangham found the system envisaged in the plan and bill as against their interest. So the conference failed from urging the Government to enact that legislation or give any publicity to that Bill[15]. This approach of the Sangham to the modernization of library system of the State continued throughout later history. Before a short period Sir C.P. Ramaswamy Aiyer had to resign and quit the State.

Attempts for Administrative Powers

In 1948 the delegates of the Sangham met the new Dewan Sri P.G. Narayanan Unnithan and impressed him with the achievements of the Sangham. The memorandum submitted by them urged the Dewan to recognize the Sangham as the spokesman and representative of all libraries in the State and to give the right to inspect the libraries, recommend for giving grant to libraries and correspond with the Government on behalf of libraries[16]. It also wanted modification and amendment of the clause 194 of the Travancore Education code dealing with the condition for giving grant to libraries[17]. The deputation pointed out that the libraries in Travancore State were under the control of different bodies such as Department of Education, City Corporation, village development authority, Devaswam and Harijan Welfare Department, and that all of them must be brought under the administrative control of one organization the Sangham[18]. In fact the objectives of the leaders were to get the Sangham accepted as the Department of Libraries. Actually at this stage or in later years the Sangham never included any professional experts in it, required for undertaking such activities or organizing a State's library system. They were mere political or social activists who came to the top position of the Sangham elected from different levels. And they wanted the Sangham to have the same character always. This is the reason why Sangham always used to comment what Kerala needs is not scientifically organized library system for information service to the people, but democratically organized system in which people's involvement will be more and which will train the people in the system of democracy[19].

Sangham also urged the new Dewan to take steps to start a Library Science Department in the University of Travancore to train librarians.

Travancore Library Advisory Committee, 1948

Impressed perhaps more by the indefatigable activities of the office bearers of the Sangham and their perseverance and selfless devotion to duty, the Dewan appointed a committee consisting of Sooranat Kunjan Pillai, Mathew M. Kuzhiveli and Sivarama Subramanya Iyer to review the work done by the Sangham and recommend the feasible assistance and encouragements to be given to the Sangham[20].

The committee strongly recommended the formulation of a planned library policy to be undertaken by government in collaboration with non-official agencies obviously meaning thereby the Sangham[21]. The compelling reasons as given by the committee was that libraries in the State were of different categories and many of them were owned by different groups including communal and religious organizations. Then there were libraries run by local authorities. Hundreds of libraries established by the labour of the enlightened village groups with the blessings and help of local patrons remained imperfectly equipped. Hence the committee urged that a well thought out library policy of Government is urgent. The committee after making observations about the defects, drawbacks and shortcomings of the functioning of various libraries recommended in favour of the demands contained in the memorandum of the Sangham. The recommendations included the doubling of the annual grant for the Sangham and authorising the Sangham to inspect libraries and recommend the award of grants to libraries. It also recommended the affiliating of all libraries including the departmental libraries of government to the Sangham and involving the Sangham also in the conducting of a course for librarians by the Education Department of State.

Due to sudden changes that came in the Government, no action was taken on this report. In 1949 Cochin State merged into Travancore to form Travancore-Cochin State. With this, all the public libraries run by Government and other village libraries which existed in Cochin also came under the control of the Sangham to be run as public libraries[22]. The Library Department, which functioned in the Cochin State was abolished. In 1956 when the Indian States were re-organized into linguistic States, Malabar region also joined the other two, that is Travancore and Cochin and the present Kerala State was formed. With the birth of Kerala, Sangham extended its activities to Malabar area also. The Sangham which had started functioning with 47 libraries as its members has now grown into a wide movement with more than two thousand libraries under it.

REFERENCES

1. Kerala Granthasala Sangham. *Granthasala Manual.* Trivandrum: the author, 1967.
2. Panikkar, PN, Ed. Keralathile granthasala prasthanam, Trivandrum: *Steps,* 1982.
3. Kerala Granthasala Sangham. *Op. cit.,* 1.
4. Raman Nair, R. Emergence of organised library movement in Kerala. *International Library Movement.* Vol. 14, No. 2, 1992.
5. Ramanujan Nair, R. *Library Movement in Kerala,* Trivandrum: Writers Club, 1974.
6. Kerala, Legislature, Secretariat of -. Kerala Public Libraries Bill 1971: Background materials. Trivandrum: the author, 1972.

7. Panikkar, P.N. Library Movement in Kerala. *Herald of Library Science,* 1974, Vol.13, No.3-4.
8. Kerala, Legislature. *Op. cit.,* 6.
9. Panikkar. *Op. cit.,* 2.
10. *Ibid.*
11. Brief history of Granthasala Sangham. In *Granthasala Sangham's Silver Jubilee Souvenir,* Trivandrum: KGS, 1971.
12. Panikkar, *Op. cit.,* 2.
13. Brief history. *Op. cit.,* 11.
14. Panikkar, *Op. cit.,* 2.
15. Raman Nair, R. Keralathile granthasala prasthanam. Cochin: *Veekshanam.* 11.12.87.
16. Ramanujan Nair. *Op. cit.,* 5.
17. Brief history. *Op. cit.,* 11.
18. Ramanujan Nair, *Op. cit.,* 5.
19. Raman Nair, R. Kerala Granthasala Sangham Lakshyam Nediyo. Cochin: *Veekshanam.* 12.8.87.
20. Ramanujan Nair, *Op. cit.,* 5.
21. Travancore, All Travancore Library Association, Committee on -. Report. Trivandrum; the author, 1948.
22. Panikkar. *Op. cit.,* 7.

7

MEANS OR ENDS

The foundation of an institution is built according to a plan convenient and acceptable to the forces that worked behind the evolution of that institution. For any purpose totally or partially different from the original ones structures different from those that the foundations can hold will be required. Adopting the same base or accommodating different structure in the same foundation will cause inefficiency or weakness in any system.

The people's library movement which the Sangham had organized came into existence and developed due to some specific reasons which were present throughout the first-half of the nineteenth century[1]. The following can be considered as main causes.

* With the growth of education, interest in books and reading habits of the people developed. Their desire to have some reading materials within easily approachable distance was quite natural.
* Huge storms were blowing on in the political and social spheres of life. Revolutionary movements were at their peak. All people were curious to know the daily happenings. Newspapers were beyond the power of most to afford and so they thought about reading rooms or small libraries in their community.
* Even though Government popularised education which was the cause for the people's curiosity for news and their desire to know more and more and read extensively, Government was not able to spread the library service as fast as formal educational services are spread; so as to satisfy this requirement of the people.
* Every community wanted to have a place for political chit

chat, entertainment and cultural activities during their leisure time. Government at those times never thought of providing these facilities.

Nature of People's Libraries

People by themselves started organizing small clubs or centres which were named with one or more terms of 'library', 'reading room', 'arts club', 'arts and sports club', etc. They were very simple and the purposes were also simple. They provided newspapers, light reading materials, two or three desks and benches and a little space to play cards or chat. In most of the villages and small village towns they sprang up, and the surrounding community associated their cultural and literary activities and sports and games to these institutions. By organizing these activities the people especially the youth of the area got themselves trained in the organization and administration of democratic institutions in miniature form.

The local political leaders and social activists found in them a base from where they can more easily spread their ideas and collect more workers and supporters. They also found in them an organization in their community which can permit the involvement in its working, the novices of politics to get them trained in the working of democratic institutions. So political workers from all parties joined these institutions, actively participated in their working and influenced their activists in nearby places where there was no libraries, to start such institutions. The administrative structure of the libraries were also formed very much like that of local units of political parties functioning on democratic lines. They were managed by a committee elected by all the members of the unit. It goes without saying that in election, members contested in groups or panels meant for all offices; supported by or affiliated to different political parties and actually it was a democratic system in miniature.

Library System Under Sangham

Gradually the movement formed the State level union of these units with District and Taluk level committees very much like any political party. The leaders of this movement claim the library system envisaged by this union that is the Granthasala Sangham, as the most efficient one and its administrative set-up on democratic line as unique among any library set-up existing throughout the world[2]. They also opine it as the major factor responsible for the significant achievements of the Sangham.

How far these claims are true. To evaluate the system of the Sangham we have to know how far it could achieve the objectives of a public library system. We have to compare it with the guidelines and systems evolved; experimented and prooved to be efficient by experts. With the presentation of a Model Library Act at All Asia Educational Conference at Benaras in 1930 a concept of far advanced system for Public Library service had been evolved by Dr. S.R. Ranganathan. Through its various revisions after observing the working of systems which adopted that model, Ranganathan has perfected the concept and the system to such an extent that it still seems far advanced in these days of technological revolution. For Kerala also Ranganathan prepared Library Bills and Development Plans based on this perfected system and concept. Government always tried to implement system suggested by Ranganathan or systems very similar to his one. But whenever such proposals came Sangham objected them saying that the existing system of the Sangham is more better and fit for the development of Library service in Kerala than those envisaged by any other bills or plans. The leaders of the Sangham always urged the Government to accept its system and its administrative set-up as the basis for any library legislation.

The Sangham in the manner in which it was constituted and in its functioning, is different from any other library association or library system existing anywhere[3]. The Sangham's constitution and rules were also entirely different from any such library legislation. Hence for considering the worth of the library system and legislation suggested by Sangham, for considering how far the present Kerala Public Library Act has accepted these principles and to what effect; we have to examine the constitution, functions and achievements of the Sangham.

Objectives of the Sangham

The objectives of the Sangham as per its last constitution and rules were[4]:

* To function as the central organization for all libraries in the state;
* To work for the improvement of the existing libraries;

* To render all possible help for adult education;
* To prevent the neo-literates from relapsing into illiteracy and provide facilities to the educated to read and acquire knowledge;
* To work for the establishment of a library department in the State;
* To undertake publication activities helpful to library workers;
* To conduct training courses for library workers; and
* To start a Central Library in each Taluk.

In the beginning Sangham affiliated all libraries without any minimum standards. But later it put some restrictions which were mainly due to the directions given by the Government related to the sanction of library grants. Libraries to be fit for affiliation should have minimum 600 books, 5 periodicals, 3 dailies, a room for its use and a few furniture items[5].

Organization of the Sangham

The Sangham has a hierarchical pattern of organization. The various bodies which its constitution provides are as follows[6]:

Individual member libraries, to whatever grade they belong are autonomous institutions working according to the model library rules prescribed by the Sangham and accepted by them. Each library is managed by a committee elected by the General body of all members of the library. All the libraries of the Taluk are co-ordinated by a Taluk union. Each library in the Taluk can send two representatives to the Taluk union and such representatives of all libraries in the Taluk constitute the general body of Taluk union. The General Body elects a working committee of 9 members. The Taluk union has a president, a vice-president, a secretary and a joint secretary. The administration of the Taluk union is vested in the working committee. The source of revenue for the Taluk union is 36 per cent of the subscriptions paid by the individual libraries to the Sangham. The Taluk Library union keeps a close surveillance of the working of each library in its jurisdiction and ensures that the libraries maintain records and generally observe in its working, the rules laid down by the Sangham. It also helps the establishment of libraries by local initiative and in strengthening the existing libraries in the Taluk. The District Committee supervises the work of all the Taluk unions. It is constituted of the representatives of the Taluk unions in the District on the basis of one representative per

Taluk, 3 members of the Bharana Samithi from that District and two persons nominated by the Bharana Samithi of the Sangham from a panel of 5 names proposed by the elected members of the committee. The District committee functions as the liaison between the Taluk unions and the Sangham. It receives from Sangham twenty per cent of the subscriptions paid by libraries and also ad-hoc grants for the conduct of conferences etc.

Granthasala Sangham coordinates, harmonizes, directs and leads the numerous libraries in the State. The General Body of the Taluk union while electing for its working committee also elects representatives for the General Body of the Sangham on the basis of one member for every 10 libraries in a Taluk. It is stipulated that there should be not less than 3 and not more than 7 members for each Taluk. The representatives so elected along with life members and vice-patrons constitute the General Body of the Sangham.

The General Body elects members of the Bharana Samithi of the Sangham on the basis of 3 members for each revenue district. Two members are elected by the General Body from among life members and vice-patrons. These elected representatives nominate 6 persons from among renowned educationists, literary men, lawyers, social workers etc. There are also two members on the Bharana Samithi nominated by the Government and one member nominated by the University of Kerala. Thus except 3 members, all members of the Bharana Samithi are elected or nominated by the representatives of libraries. The controlling role of library workers in the affairs of Sangham is evident from this. Professional expertise has no place in the system.

The Bharana Samithi elects a president, 2 vice-presidents, a general secretary, 2 joint secretaries and a treasurer who along with other 4 elected members constitute the working committee. The Bharana Samithi is the Chief Executive and policy making body of the Sangham. The working committee concerns itself with the administrative matters within the framework of policy laid down by the Bharana Samithi. The Sangham has a secretariat which is headed by the General Secretary who is assisted by Administrative Assistants, Superintendent, Accountant and other staff. The Government have sanctioned an annual grant of Rs. one lakh for the maintenance of the office and for the organizational work. The other sources of revenue are 44 per cent of the subscriptions from the libraries, sale proceeds of publications and private donations.

Achievements of the Sangham

Sangham was an unique movement. Its contributions to Kerala's politics and culture are immense. In involving the people and in mass appeal, it reached the levels no Government project on the cultural field could ever attain. The most outstanding achievement of the Sangham was the quiet but enduring contribution it made towards establishing grassroots of democracy in the State. During the period of its existence nearly 75,000 workers became actively connected with the movement during different times. Moulding the social workers is an extraordinary activity. The youngmen and women who dedicated their time to this movement got a feeling of achievement when they saw their cooperative effort taking shape and yielding beneficient results to their community. Thus they developed the qualities of leadership. With this training and confidence hundreds of them later became efficient leaders of many political parties and organizations. Some of the persons who became ministers in Kerala, got their initial training in social and political work in Sangham.

As a system for training the members of the society in democratic government and as a system for cultural activities of the society Sangham was excellent[7]. But as a system which is intended to give the library and information service to the members of the information based society in the days of knowledge explosion; Sangham was totally inappropriate. Its concept of library and information service has become obsolete[8].

Demoralization of the Movement

During the period of its existence Sangham has slowly altered the attitude of the people towards libraries from the earlier existing concept and the concept that was evolving parallel to the needs of the society. Due to the publicity given by Sangham to its activities and methods, people began to consider public library as a place where the community can utilize their leisure time and from where they can organize social and cultural activities. They envisaged public library as something between a sports and arts club and a reading room. They began to consider it as a place to discuss, know about and get trained in practical politics. The election to the offices of library can be called miniature or mock political elections imitating elections to parliament and legislature. As the activists of Sangham claimed; the system was democratic and it gave training to the people in democracy. But how much per cent of the people are able to involve and get training or closely watch these activities; remains to be assessed[9]. Actually it is only the educated upper class who are dominant in every society that participated in the governance of this system[10].

Defects of the System Proposed by Sangham

The findings of the Ashok Mehta Committee and many other committees appointed by various State governments to go into the failures and partial success of Panchayati Raj institutions on the following aspects should however be an eye opener to the protagonists of elected bodies. The following reasons were attributed to the failure of Panchayati Raj institutions:

* Political factionalism developed and diluted all developmental work;
* Funds given to them were grossly inadequate and they were hit by financial crunch; and
* The attention given to Panchayat institutions by Government is niggardly.

What is said of the Panchayati Raj Institution is applicable to the elected library authorities also. Political factionalism is bound to creep into ranks of local library authorities constituted by election[11]. In 1970's Sangham faced these situations to the maximum[12]. In the elections for different offices of the Sangham conducted in 1976 the contest was purely on political party basis. In 17 Taluks the elections ended in street fight between the different parties which contested and there was total confusion and chaos[13]. So the State Government was forced to take over the Sangham and its administration.

Eventhough Sangham's system is a purely democratic system, a system which can create such a chaotic situation, and which is not having continuation of responsibility is not fit for a library and information system for the people which requires too much planning, specialized staff and finance. Quality of material with which a machine is made is of no value if the product of the machine is not up to the mark. It is not the democratic system for library service which matters here, but the library and information services which is to sustain democracy about which we are to be concerned[14]. In the forthcoming chapters we shall discuss the objectives and functions of the public library in the present day society and the principles behind public library legislation and the systems evolved, experimented and generally accepted as able to achieve these aims and objectives.

REFERENCES

1. Raman Nair, R. Keralathile granthasala prasthanam. Cochin: *Veekhanam,* 11.8.1987.
2. Panikkar, P.N. Kerala Granthasala Sangham. In *Granthasala directory.* Trivandrum: KGS, 1964.
3. Kerala, Legislature, Secretariat of -. Kerala Public Library Bill 1985: Background materials. Trivandrum: the author, 1986.
4. Kerala Granthasala Sangham. Constitution and Rules. Trivandrum: the author, 1975.
5. Kerala, legislature. *Op. cit.,* 3.
6. Kerala, Granthasala Sangham. *Op. cit.,* 4.
7. Raman Nair, R. Gramangalil vijnana vitaranam. *Trivandrum Vijnana Kairali,* 1988, Vol. 14, No. 8.
8. *Ibid.*
9. Raman Nair, R. Kerala Granthasala Sangham lakshyam nediyo Cochin: *Veekshnam,* 12.8.1987.
10. *Ibid.*
11. Hashmi, Syd Ali. Library legislations in India. In ILA Conference papers. New Delhi: ILA, 1983.
12. Sreeraj, B. Kakshi rastreeyam takartha oru mahaprasthanam. Calicut: *Mathrubhoomi* Weekly, 26.6.1982.
13. Panikkar, P.N. Granthasala Prasthanathe sarkar takarkaruthu. Trivandrum: *Kerala Kaumudhi,* 26.6.1985.
14. Raman Nair, R. Kerala Granthasala Sangham; A unique experiment on people's participation in information system development. Proceedings of South Indian History Congress. Kalady, SSUS, 1998.

8

INFLUENCES THROUGH SPACE

In the previous chapters we have done a rapid survey of the evolution of libraries and the customs traditions and laws governing them in Kerala from the hoary past through four of the five phases of their evolution. At the national level also a parallel development more magnificent and broad can be traced during these periods. But that is out of our scope of study.

But in the fifth phase which we have to survey, Kerala cannot be studied as an independent compartment. During this phase Kerala is not a sovereign State. It has become a part of the Indian union. Legislative powers of the State is limited. Enactment of any legislation and building up of any system is to be done in consultation with the Union Government. The system and legislation should also be framed so as to become an efficient part of the total system of the nation so that sharing of the national resources becomes possible and smooth.

The fifth phase falls in an entirely different setting of library history than the past ones. Many global forces have worked towards legislation based highly specialized public library systems[1]. The development in the sociological thought has shattered all the social barriers and forced the society to move towards a socialistic pattern. It implied equal right to all for free public library and information service. It has to be free and supported by legislation because the poorest in the community should get as much that service as the richest. The developments in political thoughts influenced the equal distribution of sovereignty among all adults of the nation through adult franchise. To make this full and democracy safe and beneficial, it is essential to keep one and all of the citizens furnished with correct information, to provide opportunity for independent judgement on the basis of perusal of all possible views. In its own interest democracy is obliged to provide free and extensive information service to the people. Industrialization has also made the people's information systems very important. Population pressure has already gone beyond the capacity of the natural and near natural resources to feed, clothe and house for all the people. Therefore, there is need for intelligent conservation of all available resources by everybody, maximising the production of natural and near natural commodities by intensive cultivation and the transformation of non-consumable raw materials into beneficial commodities through technology of ever increasing sophistication. These required continuous dissemination of latest scientific ideas and knowledge among one and all of the people. This is development of the human resources of the nation. As the Sangham classic Tirukkural says the wealth of all wealth is the wealth of human resources. This makes library and information service the primary responsibility of the State. For the social political and industrial development of a nation universal education is a necessity. Experience throughout the world has proved that free education for all not backed by free library and information service for all is like a mud house without a roof.

Revolutionary Changes in Library Concept

Knowledge explosion, innovation and speed in printing technology, resultant huge mass of printed materials produced every minute, and dependence on information by all aspects of human progress have forced the library to adopt itself quickly and efficiently to these changing situations. Those which failed to change remained mere curiosity shops.

Through a very fast process of evolution during this century, service oriented libraries of modern world have changed to a state where they are more or less different service outlets, each outlet having the common attitude and approach, common aims and objectives and more or less uniform organizational and administrative set-ups with the whole information resources of the nation at its disposal for dissemination[2]. In this world of fast changing technologies and knowledge explosion, the public library and information service will be futile unless it is organized by staff with proper professional specialization. So a specialized profession also evolved for this particular work.

In 1927 Kenyan Committee reported that the public interest in libraries has greatly increased and we believe there is now a far healthier belief in the value of knowledge and in the importance of intellectual life in all busy centres of national activity than in any previous period of history[3]. In such centres the public library is no longer regarded as a means of providing casual recreation of an unimportant character; it is recognized as an engine of great potentialities for national welfare and as an essential foundation for the progress in education and culture without which no people can hold its own in the struggle for existence.

The developments in the library and information service scene that is fastly achieving new dimensions around the world influenced India also. The movements for evolving, establishing and coordinating library systems in India at the national level and at State level were quickened. A study of the library movement in Kerala in the modern period which we classify as fifth phase cannot disregard the direct and indirect influences from these national level movements and the developments in other States. In this chapter we attempt a brief survey of these developments around Kerala, so that their inter-relationship will become apparent and the library movement in Kerala will appear in perspective as a part of the developments in the nation as a whole.

Even before India achieved independence; from the part of the Government there were attempts to improve the public information system. Bombay Government's attempt to register and support libraries in 1808, Government of India's Press and Registration of Books Act 1867 and the Imperial Library Act of 1902 were some of them[4].

Baroda Public Library System

Eventhough Visakam Tirunal Maharaja of Travancore was the first ruler to issue consolidated rules related to all aspects of Public Library System defining the purpose and methods of organizing them the credit of having initiated the first well articulated system of public libraries under Governmental order in the country goes to Sri Sayajirao Gaekwad of Baroda State. The Maharaja an enlightened ruler had in 1906 initiated a scheme of compulsory primary education, the first State in the country to sponsor such a progressive measure. He was of the opinion that the State aided free public libraries are absolutely essential for continuing education. Money spent on few years of compulsory primary education would go waste unless there is an adequate provision for follow-up work as a life-long process[5]. Only free public library service can keep mass, literate after their formal education is over. Maharaja linked up primary education with a free public library system as a matter of rule.

The library movement in Baroda started in 1910 when primary education also was made free and compulsory[6]. Maharaja invited Mr. M.A. Borden, an American Librarian in 1910, to introduce a scientifically organized library system. With the assistance of Borden the Maharaja established the State Central Library and a planned network of free public libraries throughout the State. A separate department of libraries was also established. They introduced open access system for all libraries. First library school was started in 1910 by Borden to train the professionals who are required for running these libraries. A library science journal was also started in 1912. The result of these activities are visible even today in these regions. Even today 85 per cent of the people of Baroda have library facilities. But after the Maharaja there was no follow-up work. Maharaja was very much like Sri S.R. Ranganathan a man ahead of his time and our time also. It took exactly 42 years of struggle in this modern world for Kerala to enact library legislation. Even then it could not envisage a system as efficient as that Baroda have in the beginning of the century. No democratic ruler of Kerala showed a benevolent attitude to this social legislation like Sayajirao.

Model Library Act, 1930

The concept of legislation for public library systems as it stands today is a contribution of Dr. S.R. Ranganathan to the world of libraries. In the 1920's nowhere in the world a perfect library system as conceived by Dr. S.R. Ranganathan existed. Eventhough United Kingdom had the most efficient and earliest legislation for libraries in the modern world, the library network extending from village library through intermediary levels of district, State and zonal levels to State and National Central Libraries, coordinated by a national agency is not conceived by the U.K. legislation. In 1927 Kenyan Committee had pointed out that library authorities grew rapidly in an uncoordinated fashion and standards of library service varied greatly between various library authorities and areas[7].

In 1925 while sailing back home after a tour to England, Ranganathan was thinking about a library legislation for India without the defects seen in U.K. legislation. He worked out on it and by 1930 drafted a Model Library Act[8]. At this time Prof. P. Seshadri of Banaras Hindu University asked him to be the secretary of the Library Service Session of the First All-Asia Educational Conference which was to be held in Benaras in 1930. This provided him an opportunity to place the draft Model Act for discussion. The Draft Act presented by Ranganathan and the originality and precision of his plan impressed the participants. A complete session of the conference was devoted to a detailed discussion of the several clauses in the Act and the amendments suggested were recorded[9]. This Act was of compulsory nature in as much as it was obligation on the part of the local bodies to levy library cess and on the part of the government to give grants. It was in this conference at Benaras that the establishment of a public library system and pooling up the total information resources of the nation on a legal basis for the common good is for the first time contemplated and planted in the minds of a gathering which included eminent educationists and librarians. This model act is the seed out of which modern library legislation grew.

Contributions of Dr. S.R. Ranganathan

For library legislation in the constituent states Ranganathan has drafted on the occasions specified below six Model Library Bills and plans, each an improvement over earlier one[10].

Place of Discussion/Publication

- 1930 In the First All-Asia Educational Conference at Banaras. It was also published in his book *Five Laws of Library Science.*
- 1942 *Fifth All India Library Conference,* Bombay, also published as book by ILA.
- 1950 Published in his Report: Library Development Plan: Thirty Year Programme for India with Draft Library Bills for Union and the States.
- 1957 A revised Model Bill in the new edition of *Five Laws of Library Science.*
- 1964 Published in the Quarterly *Library Science with a Slant to Documentation'.*
- 1972 Model Public Libraries Act revised after the evaluation of the working of existing acts was published in the book *Public Library System* edited by him.

Based on these Model Bills and Acts and the requirements assessed from the data supplied by concerned regions Ranganathan prepared Draft Public Library Bills, Acts and Development Plans for the following constituent States. Most of these Bills were handed over to the concerned Ministers. Others were published in the concerned States[11].

1946 Central Provinces
1947 Travancore
1947 Cochin
1947 Bombay
1949 United Provinces
1953 Hyderabad
1957 Madhya Pradesh
1957 Andhra Pradesh
1958 West Bengal
1958 Uttar Pradesh
1959 Kerala
1961 Mysore
1964 Assam

In 1948 the Government of India appointed a committee to examine the provision for the National Central Library. In order to make the work of the committee proceed along constructive lines, S.R. Ranganathan who was one if its members drafted a Union Library Bill and presented it at the second meeting of the Committee held on 14 May 1948; which was generally approved by the Committee[12]. But no further action was taken by the Government. Sir Maurice Gwyer, the then Vice-Chancellor of the University of Delhi, a person who was highly interested in Library Development asked Ranganathan not to feel dejected at the indifference of the Government and published his plan including the Draft Union Bill from the University of Delhi so that any future Ministry if interested could make use of that Bill and Plan[13]. Ranganathan published a revised Union Bill in his second edition of *Five Laws* in 1957. The influence of these works by Ranganathan in Indian Library movement was tremendous. In most of the States the Library Associations, Legislators or other interested social activists urged the Government to enact library legislation on the Model suggested by Ranganathan. Everywhere movement for legislation became strong.

Delivery of Books Act, 1954

In 1954 Government of India enacted the Delivery of Books (Public Libraries) Act which was amended in 1956 to include newspapers also[14]. The Act required the publishers to deliver a copy each to the National Library at Calcutta and to three other public libraries which were declared as book depositories in the country. This Act has facilitated the compilation of Indian National Bibliography.

Sinha Committee, 1957

In 1957 the Government of India constituted an Advisory Committee for libraries under the Chairmanship of Sri K.P. Sinha. The committee in its comprehensive report recommended for[15]:

* Enactment of a Central Library Act by Government of India;
* Enactment of a State Library Act by each State;
* Authority for local bodies to levy a library cess as surcharge on property tax; and
* Provision for the Government of India grant equal to the library cess in a State.

Draft Library Bill, 1963

Consequent upon the recommendations made by the Advisory Committee for Libraries, the Government of India in 1960 appointed a committee for drafting a library bill under the Chairmanship of Dr. S.M. Sen[16]. The committee submitted its draft bill to the Ministry of Education in 1963. The Bill was then circulated to the various State Governments and professional organizations for their comment. This bill provided for the establishment, maintenance and development of public libraries in the State. The Bill also provided that there should be State Library Authority to advise the State Government in regard to the promotion and development of library service in the State. The Minister for Education and the Director of State Library Directorate were to be Chairman and Secretary respectively of the Authority. There was also provision for a Standing Library Committee to advise the State Library Directorate in all technical matters relating to the libraries and to make recommendations to the State Library Authority on matters relating to library development in the State. The Bill provided that every local body in a district should levy in its area a library tax in the form of surcharge on property tax not being less than six paise for every rupee.

National Level Institutions

Enactment of Khuda Baksh Oriental Public Library Act 1969 made that library a national institution and appointed a new board for this library with Governor of Bihar as Chairman[17]. Founded by Khan Bahadur Khuda Bhaksha, this library contained thousands of rare Arabic, Persian and other manuscripts. The Raja Ram Mohan Roy Library

Foundation was established in 1972 as an autonomous organization sponsored and fully financed by Government of India's Ministry of Education and Culture to support the programme of public library development initiated by State governments. It is governed by a body of 21 members with Central Minister for Education and Culture as Chairman. There is also an administrative committee. The country is divided into four zones and four zonal offices are there.

National Library of India Act, 1976

In 1976 the Government of India passed another Act namely the National Library of India Act 1976 which provides for the establishment of a statutory board which will take over from the Government of India the administration of the National Library[18]. The Board will be known as the National Library Board. The Board shall consists of 30 members, three of them being there by virtue of their office, thirteen including a Chairman will be nominated by Government of India, two persons to be elected by the Lok Sabha and one from the Council of States, three persons to be nominated by the Governments of the States by rotation, four persons to represent the Universities in India, one will be nominated by the Indian Library Association, two to be elected by the offices and staff of the National Library and one person to be nominated by the Government of West Bengal. The Director of National Library will be the Member-Secretary. Clause 11 empowered the Board to constitute an executive council consisting of nine members. The Director of the library shall be its Chairman and other members shall be appointed by the Board partly from among members of the Board and partly from outside. The executive council shall exercise such powers and perform such duties as the Board may delegate to it.

Movement for Library Legislation in States

The writings of Dr. S.R. Ranganathan his Model Acts, Bills and Library Development Plans influenced in the States; movements for library development and legislation and gave them strength and clearcut principles. Whenever, it became possible Ranganathan personally went to the States and gave expert advice and support to these activities. Till now in eight of the States the move for library legislation has become fruitful and all of them except Kerala totally or partially accepted the principles and plan developed by Dr. S.R. Ranganathan.

Madras Public Library Act, 1949

It was the untiring efforts of Ranganathan that resulted in the enactment of the first library legislation in India at Madras. In 1946 Mr. Avinasilingam Chettiyar, a student of Ranganathan, became Education Minister of Madras. Ranganathan directly discussed with the Minister his Draft Bill for Madras. Minister got it examined through Law Department. Some modifications were made in it by legal experts. The Minister then piloted the Bill in the Legislature which was enacted as the official Bill of the Government. Thus we got the Madras Public Library Act which was assented by the Governor General in 29th January 1949 which ushered in a new phase in library history of India[19].

Hyderabad Public Library Act, 1955

The second State that enacted library law in India was Hyderabad[20]. This Act emerged in an atmosphere charged with enthusiasm for the library movement and it was the result of pressure exerted by a group of enthusiasts which included the State's Minister of Education. The draft bill prepared by Ranganathan was discussed in a seminar directed by him in which Members of the Legislature, officers of Government, Education Minister and Chief Minister were present. Everyone including Education Minister was convinced with the bill. They presented it in the Legislature and was enacted in 1955.

Andhra Pradesh Public Library Act, 1960

Andhra Pradesh was the third State to enact library legislation in 1960[21]. A peculiar situation arose in the State with the bifurcation of the then composite Madras State in 1955 and the merging of the several districts from the disintegrated Hyderabad State. So two Library Acts were in operation in the districts of Andhra Pradesh; one Madras Library Act 1949 and the other Hyderabad Public Libraries Act 1955. To remove the anomaly created by the provisions of the two different Acts, the Government consulted Ranganathan and according to his suggestions enacted the Andhra Pradesh Public Library Act in 1960.

Karnataka Public Library Act, 1965

Karnataka was the fourth State to bring a Library Act into operation[22]. In 1962 Ranganathan having retired from the North established DRTC at Bangalore. He also founded the Karnataka Library Association with Mr. Vaikunta Baliga, Speaker of Karnataka Legislative Assembly as its President. Due to the request of the Association Government set up a Library Committee to draft a library bill and development plan for the State with Ranganathan as Chairman and Education Minister also as a member. The committee provided Ranganathan maximum freedom to draft a comprehensive library bill with some new classes not provided in earlier acts but necessitated by the later developments. Ranganathan submitted the bill for consideration of Government. The draft bill was accepted by the Government and enacted into Karnataka Public Library Act in 1965.

Karnataka Public Library Act is considered as a great advance over the Madras and Andhra Pradesh Library Acts. It has more realistic financial classes. The Act has created Karnataka Library Service. This provision had virtually nationalised the library service and the will.

Maharashtra Public Library Act, 1967

Maharashtra Government through its officials prepared a draft library bill based on some earlier bills of Ranganathan. The bill was enacted into Maharashtra Public Libraries Act in 1967[23]. The Act made certain departure from the earlier Acts as it did not provide for library cess, but provided for library grants by the government for maintenance and development of libraries.

West Bengal, Manipur, Kerala and Haryana Acts

West Bengal was the fifth State to enact public library legislation. It has carefully studied the working of the existing acts and accordingly revised the bill prepared for that State by Ranganathan in 1958 which was enacted as West Bengal Public Libraries Act 1979[24]. After that Manipur has enacted a legislation. By enacting Kerala Public Library Act in May 1989 Kerala became the seventh State to have Library legislation. But it followed a totally different pattern than other States. Haryana enacted Library Legislation in September 1989 and it accepted most of the principles of Ranganathan and the good aspects of the other existing Library Acts.

Chattopadhyaya Committee, 1986

While constituting Rajaram Mohan Roy Library Foundation,

Government entrusted it the work of formulating a National Policy on Library and Information System. In 1984 the Foundation submitted a draft policy[25]. In 1985 Indian Library Association also submitted another draft policy. So the Government of India set up a committee under the Chairmanship of Sri P.P. Chattopadhyaya for considering these drafts and for the formulation of a final document on National Library and Information Policy in the context of the expanding library movement. The committee submitted its report in May 1986. The committee has stressed that establishing, maintaining and strengthening free public library service in the country and enabling libraries to work as a system is the most important task before the Government[26]. The committee has also suggested that the Central Government should revise the Model Public Library Bill in the light of the experience gained and the developments happened after its preparation and urge upon the States to enact uniform legislation based on this revised Model Act so that national level coordination will become possible. All libraries in the State should form part of a network extending from the community library of the village through intermediary levels to the district and to the State Central Library. This State network should eventually be connected with the national level network.

The recommendations of Chattopadhyaya Committee are based on the concepts of most advanced principles behind public library systems existing throughout the world. The objectives of the socialist information systems for the people is to pool the total information resources of the nation and make it available to all the citizens in an equal and unbiased way. It also makes it possible for anyone poor or wealthy to get any recorded information available anywhere in the nation or outside, through the information service outlet maintained by the State near his home, in his village or town. But to us there is actually nothing new in these recommendations. S.R. Ranganathan has continuously suggested the same system since 1948 in his writings and his library development plans. He has always stressed that Government should give high priority to public library system legislation because it is the only system which makes for the people the access to information easy and free.

REFERENCES

1. Ranganathan, S.R. Philosophy of free book service for all. In Ranganathan, Ed. *Free Book Service For All: An International Survey*. Bombay: Asia, 1968.

2. Raman Nair R. Gramangalil Vijnanavitaranam. Trivandrum: *Vijnanakairali,* 1988, Vol. 14, No. 8.
3. United Kingdom, Education, Board of -, Public Libraries, Committee on–. Report. London: HMSO, 1927.
4. India, Education and Youth Services, Ministry of -, Libraries, Advisory Committee for-. Report. New Delhi: the author, 1957.
5. Deshpande, K.S. Library legislation in India. In Rout, R.K. *Library Legislation in India: Problems and Prospects.* New Delhi: Reliance, 1986.
6. *Ibid.*
7. United Kingdom. *Op. cit.,* 3.
8. Kaula, P.N. Some facts about library legislation in India. In Rout, *Library Legislation in India.*
9. Gopinath, M.A. History of library legislation in India. In Ranganathan and Neela Meghan, Ed. *Public Library System;* Bangalore: SREL, 1972.
10. Ranganathan, S.R. India. In Ranganathan, Ed. *Free Book Service For All.*
11. *Ibid.*
12. Gopinath. *Op. cit.,* 9.
13. Ranganathan, S.R. *Library Development Plan: Thirty Year Programme for India with Draft Library Bills for the Union and the Constituent States.* Delhi: University of Delhi, 1950.
14. Srivastava, Shyam Nath. Library legislation in India. *International Library Review,* 1972, 4, p.329-339.
15. India. *Op. cit.,* 4.
16. Misra, V.P. Library legislation in India. In ILA Conference papers, New Delhi: ILA, 1983.
17. Srivastava. *Op. cit.,* 14.
18. Goil, N.K. National Library of India: A desired perspective for 1980's. In Proceedings of the seminar on the Role of National Library in India. Calcutta: NLEA, 1979.
19. Kaula. *Op. cit.,* 8.
20. *Ibid.*
21. Deshpande. *Op. cit.,* 5.
22. Khan, H.A. Karnataka Public Library Act: A critical review of its implementation. In Rout. *Library Legislation in India.* I.
23. Konnur, M.B. Public Library Services and Library Act in Maharashtra. In Rout. *Library Legislation in India.*
24. Roy, Dipak Kumar. Library legislation in West Bengal. In Rout. *Library Legislation in India.*
25. Rajaram Mohan Roy Library Foundation. *National Policy on Library and Information System.* Calcutta: the author, 1984.
26. India, Education and Culture, Ministry of -, National Library and Information System, Committee on -. Report. New Delhi: the author, 1986.

9

GOALS AND OBJECTIVES

Libraries of all kinds, during thousands of years of their existence have had a common objective which has never been contested. It is collection, preservation and dissemination of knowledge. The library has been created by actual necessities of civilization. It was and it is a necessary unit of the social fabric. Culture must transcend the individual, for it is essentially through a social cumulation of experience whereby the men of each generation possess potentially, at least all that their predecessors have ever learned[1]. Recording these experiences in documents is a social mechanism for preserving the racial memory, and library a social apparatus for transferring this to the consciousness of the individuals.

Progress which we often tend to attribute to the achievements of the few brilliant teams, derives in fact from the resolve and competence of a whole population. Culture and science must therefore be distributed universally. It is only an educated people properly informed of new advances which will produce the architects of developments[2]. The latter will be powerless without the help of very large sectors of population able to understand the mechanisms of development and to take an active part in it. The two instruments which supplement the work of education to this end are on the one hand libraries with resultant dissemination of information and on the other, information designed for the popularization of different fields of knowledge which is provided through books journals and the nonprint and audio-visual media.

Support for Adjustment to Changes

The speed at which the advances in our science and technology is occurring at present has broadened the scope and elevated the level of library's activities in modern civilization. The fast development of science and technology has caused new socio-cultural pattern to emerge with turbulent changes in goals, pursuits and priorities in all facets of life of man on earth. Change is not a new phenomenon. We have been witnessing it from time immemorial. But now we are in a phase of exploding change – with personal lives being torn apart, the existing social order crumbling, and fantastic new way of life emerging on the horizon – asking the very largest of questions about our future; is not merely a matter of intellectual curiosity[3]. It is a matter of survival. This gives a new dimension to libraries, especially what we call public libraries in this new environment, for public library is the only social institution which can make the majority of society to adjust with the current trends, to develop correct attitudes, and to be aware of the consequences of wrong policies.

The goals and objectives of public library have undergone revision and re-assessment through centuries and have now been considered as the institutions which have to play very important role in the political, social, educational and economic progress of a country. In the introduction of the Report on Library Development Plan for Kerala Ranganathan says; library service is a social necessity[4]. It is an essential help to the steady development of social well-being. The library should be the heart from which every development in a community radiates and gets irradiated. It must be a social and intellectual centre of each locality. It is the community's cultural deposit for all its literary remains, a medium for the transmission of the distinctive culture of the community and a source for historical research.

Political Role

Library service is a necessity in a democracy. We are striving to attain a socialistic pattern of democracy. Democracy is impossible unless the citizens have free access to correct information. It also needs access to all points of view. It further needs the progressive sharpening of intellect in one and all. Above all it needs the sublimation of the lower emotions in the leaders as well as the followers. These are the very foundation of safe political life. These form the necessary corrective power in the management of political affairs. The public library is now recognized to be an impartial agency for the promotion of healthy political life. Its duty is to place before one and all truly balanced literature on all points of view, all lines of approach and all schools of thought. This will help the people to know, defend and enjoy their rights and realize and discharge their duties in a free society. Thomas Jefferson has rightly said that "the people of a country would never consent to the destruction of their liberties if they were informed, and nothing would do more good towards making them informed than the establishment of a small public library in every village".

Educational Role

Library service is a necessity for the preservation of universal literacy and the elimination of educational waste. Our constitution calls for universal literacy. We are spending several crore in building it up. Literacy cannot be preserved unless it is continuously exercised. Universal exercise of literacy demands a free public library system. Democratic concept of education is free access to it for one and all. Democratization of education was declared as the basic principles of educational policy in independent India. Educating each and every citizen irrespective of any caste or economic differences was accepted as the responsibility of the State. But even forty years after the policy declaration 75 per cent of our people are not in a position to get full benefit from our educational institutions maintained at huge cost which is realized from their pockets also. The formal educational system which we have so far upheld has failed to go beyond a 25 per cent of our population. If education is to reach the people beyond this privileged minority; like in all other advanced countries we also have to take education in a broader sense and we have to give more importance to adult education, continuing education and distance education, than formal education. The formal education also is to be supported by some agency which provides for the continued self education of an individual after leaving the formal educational institution. We have to develop the public library system which is to give the supporting and auxiliary services to all these systems of education. Unless this is done our educational objectives will merely remain in the idea plane and our educational system will go on serving only a privileged minority; an upper class[5]. So the public library had to play a major role in the field of education.

Social Role

Public library is a people's university. It has to offer to the people of its locality materials and services that will help them to prosper in their respective professions. It has to help the people to get along in the present day world, where inventions and discoveries are flooding every day impelling man to have continuing education for professional maturity.

Public library has a great role to play in social education to prepare people for social adjustment. It also offers materials and services to the public to understand the social phenomena and thus live a successful social life and avoid social evils. It provides opportunities to the people to understand social diseases and how to control them.

Public library is a cultural centre in more than one way. It plays a vital role in collecting and preserving the cultural heritage of the locality and making it readily available to the people to enrich their cultural awareness. It attempts to reduce the cultural lag – the time taken for the innovation to become integrated into society. Public library is also a recognized agency for providing harmless but elevating leisure.

Cultural Role

It is these facts and related attitudes that provide the basis for the public libraries of today and these concepts about public library occur in the several statements of aims and objectives of public library framed by eminent library scientists and organizations throughout the world.

Definition of Objectives

The objectives of public library as enunciated by Dr. S.R. Ranganathan are as follows[6]:

* It should help the life-long self-education of one and all;
* It should furnish up-to-date facts and information to one and all;
* It should distribute in an unbiased and balanced way, all shades of recorded views and thoughts to one and all, as a help in the discharge of their political functions in respect of local, national and international affairs;
* It should contribute to productivity drive by informing top managements of the latest trends in diverse enterprises, by ploughing back into the minds of researchers, designers, and the technicians, every piece of relevant new thought promptly and pin-pointedly;
* It should provide to one and all a harmless and elevating use of leisure;
* It should preserve the literary remains of humanity for posterity,

as vehicles of culture and as source materials for antiquarian research; and

* It should work for the continued social-well-being as the agency in charge of all socialized recorded thought.

American Public Library Enquiry

Most of the later enunciations of objectives of public library also assigned to it like Ranganathan; educational, informational, political, economic, industrial cultural and antiquarian functions. American Report of the public library inquiry defines the objectives of public library as follows[7]:

* To assemble, preserve and administer books and related educational materials in organized collections, in order to promote through guidance and stimulation, an enlightened citizenship and enriched personal lives.
* To serve the community as a general centre of reliable information.
* To provide opportunity and encouragement for children, young people, men and women to educate themselves continuously.

Second part of the report discussed public affairs and citizenship vocations, aesthetic appreciation, information and research; as the fields of knowledge and interest to which public library should devote its resources. The statement concludes by outlining library means for attaining the library objectives. The means stated include kinds of materials, availability of materials, guidance, stimulation and leadership and emphasis.

The standards framed by the American Library Association for public libraries clearly highlight the aims and objectives of public libraries today. According to it the objectives of public libraries are:

* To assist people to contribute to the growth of knowledge, to make such use of knowledge as will promote personal and social well-being;
* To develop their creative and spiritual capabilities, to make them more capable in their daily occupations, to discharge political and social obligations;
* To enable them to become better members of home and community, to keep pace with progress in all fields of knowledge

and to educate themselves continually[8].

UNESCO Public Library Manifesto

The most remarkable and elaborate statement of purpose of public libraries is found in the UNESCO's Public Library Manifesto which is revised in 1972 by IFLA. It succinctly lays down the aims and objectives of public libraries in the present world. The manifesto proclaims UNESCO's belief in the public library as a living force for education, culture and information and as an essential agent for fostering of peace and understanding between people and between nations. The manifesto continues[9]: The Public Library is a practical demonstration of democracy's faith in universal education as a continuing and life long process, in the appreciation of the achievement of humanity in knowledge and culture. The public library is the principal means whereby the record of man's thoughts and ideas, and the expression of his creative imagination are made freely available to all. The public library is concerned with the refreshment of man's spirit by the provision of books for relaxation and pleasure, with assistance to the student, and with provision of uptodate technical scientific and sociological information.

Public Library Research Group

The Public Library Research Group of the London and home countries branch of the Library Association of United Kingdom set out in 1971 outlines under the headings of education, information, culture, and leisure the following objectives for public library services[10]:

Education: to foster and provide means for self-development of the individual or group at whatever stage of education, closing the gap between the individual and recorded knowledge.

Information: to bring to the individual or group accurate information quickly and in depth, particularly on topics of current concern.

Culture: to be one of the principal centres of cultural life and promote a keener participation, enjoyment and appreciation of all arts.

Leisure: to play a part in encouraging the positive use of leisure and providing materials for change and relaxation.

Some sub-objectives listed for those responsible for organizing public libraries were: to promote the use of public libraries as education agencies for the individual; to promote the creation of specialized resources; to promote the use of public libraries as information centres; to promote the use of public libraries as referral points to specialized source of information; to promote and encourage the use of public libraries as centres where individuals can take part in the arts in a positive way; to encourage the public libraries to liaise with local societies and cultural organizations fostering the creative use of leisure in the field of arts; to promote and encourage the use of public libraries as cultural information centres; to promote the provision of general leisure material for the individual; and to promote the provision of leisure and amenity services to special groups in the community.

A Unique Institution

All the statements of aims and objectives of public library discussed above assigns to it very important roles in the fields of a nation's, education, information, political and economic development, culture and leisure. There is no other substitute to this social institution which is of such importance and which can undertake the vast and varied functions the public library is expected to undertake in the present day society the character of which is tremendous and continuous development. So an adequate system of public libraries is an absolute necessity in any country like India which is wedded to socialism and parliamentary democracy and which is aiming at marvellous development in the socio-economic, educational and cultural fields. It is an admitted fact that public library service cannot be established and maintained efficiently without a properly planned and framed library legislation in the country.

REFERENCES

1. Butler, Pierce. *An Introduction to Library Science.* Chicago: Phoenix, 1933.
2. d'Olier, J.H. and Delmas, B. *Planning National Infrastructure for Documentation, Libraries and Archives.* Paris: UNESCO, 1975.
3. Tofler, Alvin. *Third Wave,* New York, NAL, 1985.
4. Ranganathan, S.R. *Library Development Plan with a Draft Library Bill for Kerala State.* Trivandrum: Government Press, 1960.
5. Raman Nair, R. Public library purpose. In *Public Library Development.* New Delhi, Ess Ess, 1994.

6. Ranganathan, S.R. Public library system and human sources. *Herald of Library Science,* 1967, Vol. 6, No. 4.
7. Leign, Robert D. *Report of the Public Library Inquiry.* New York: Columbia, 1956.
8. American Library Association, Minimum Standards for public library systems. New York: *ALA,* 1966.
9. UNESCO and IFLA. *UNESCO Public Library Manifesto.* Paris: UNESCO, 1972.
10. Public Library Research Group and Library Association. Purpose of public libraries. *Library Association Record,* 1971, Vol. 73, No. 12.

10

INFORMATION SYSTEM FOR THE PEOPLE

Dr. S.R. Ranganathan was responsible for blowing into Kerala also, the modern concept of public library as a system, which shattered the traditional independent self sufficient public library idea. When Ranganathan was the President of Indian Library Association he made extensive library tour in Kerala in 1944 and 1946. In the second tour he also participated in the library conference organized by Kerala Granthasala Sangham and gave an inspiring talk on the need for library legislation in the State. In the same year Sir C.P. Ramaswamy Aiyar, the then Dewan of Travancore requested Ranganathan to draft a library bill for Travancore[1]. Accordingly he drafted a bill. He had also appended to the bill a thirty-year library development plan for Travancore.

Library Bill for Travancore, 1947

The library bill and development plan for Travancore was sent to the Dewan. During the library tour in 1947 Ranganathan tried to discuss it with the Dewan. As the Dewan has to leave for Delhi he ordered the Director of Education to meet Ranganathan and discuss the library bill and development plan with him. Accordingly the Director of Education and the Director of Co-operative Societies met Ranganathan. They complained that thirty years for the library development suggested by him was too long[2]. They also objected many of the other classes and provisions in the bill and development plan. They lacked the interest and ideas the Dewan had on this matter.

During these visits to Kerala Ranganathan met many noted activists of social, cultural and library fields. He discussed with them the need for library legislation and influenced them to urge the government to enact a library legislation. He also gave a copy of his draft bill to

Granthasala Sangham. The bill was placed for discussion in the annual conference of the Sangham.

Sangham becomes an Impediment

Most of the participants who wanted the State to have an efficient system for library and information service to the people were fascinated by Ranganathan's plan. But the Sangham's leaders saw in the bill only a threat to their existence because if the bill was enacted it will legalize an efficient scientifically organized system for public libraries and not the Granthasala Sangham and its leadership. In a scientifically, organized library and information system, the mere cultural and entertainment activities and their organizers will be having no scope for dominance according to their will and pleasure as was possible in the existing system of the Sangham[3]. So the conference, instead of recommending the bill objected its acceptance by government and appointed a committee to modify the bill so as to accept the existing system of the Sangham and then submit it to the government. Anyhow the discussion of the bill at the conference has created an awareness among the people, of the need for a library legislation in the State.

If the Sangham has supported the bill and showed a little interest in pressurising the government to proceed quickly with the bill Kerala would have become the first State in India to have a library legislation, for C.P. Ramaswamy Aiyar the greatest of the modernising Dewans of Travancore was too much interested in library development and was intelligent enough to understand and approve Ranganathan's ideas. On his way back to Banaras, in 1947 Ranganathan met C.P. Ramaswamy Aiyar at Madras. Aiyar asked him to spend a month with him in Trivandrum about the middle of that year to discuss directly and finalize the bill. Aiyar also promised that he would surely put the bill through[4]. But Aiyar had to resign unexpectedly. Immediately the bureaucrats wrote to Ranganathan that 'we do not think that a Library Act is necessary. We have already many libraries[5]. The bureaucracy knows the right time to dispose of files in which the higher authorities are interested.

Library Bill of Cochin, 1947

On the same tour Ranganathan visited Cochin also and met its Education Minister Panampally Govinda Menon; as the Minister had invited him to discuss about library development in Cochin. When they met Menon told Ranganathan, "A few years ago, I was a student of the Law College in Madras. I was then a regular reader in your splendid library. You might not have noticed me; one of the thousands of students who came there. I was impressed by your organization and service. Your library was so charming. It had an atmosphere. One day I wrote in my diary, Cochin State must have a library like this. As soon as I became the Education Minister, I turned through the pages of my diary to refresh my memory with my dreams of youth. I also read the news about your last visit to Kerala to inaugurate the library conference and your talk on library development and legislation. So I invited you to give guidance for enacting a library legislation in Cochin. Tell me how I should proceed." In response to the request of Menon; Ranganathan after returning to Banaras prepared and sent to Cochin a draft library Bill with a thirty-year library development plan for Cochin. But before Menon could take any action, important political changes came and Travancore and Cochin were merged into a single State.

Attempts by First Communist Ministry

During the next decade government has to settle many other political and administrative problems and no considerable move came from the part of government or Sangham to enact a library legislation. During the time of the first Communist Ministry Sri E.M.S. Namboodiripad, the Chief Minister, invited Ranganathan to visit Kerala as a consultant for the development of the State library system and for drafting a bill to be introduced in the Legislature[6]. Joseph Mundasseri, the then Education Minister and an eminent literary figure of Kerala also wrote similarly[7]. Ranganathan gladly accepted the invitation and came to Kerala. He had his first meeting with the two Ministers on 6th July 1959[8]. In the meeting Mundasseri outlined the problems on which Ranganathan was expected to work. During this stay in Kerala Ranganathan had many discussions with Director of Public Instruction, Secretary for Education and other concerned higher officials on the bill and the library development plans. He visited many libraries of Kerala to study the situation. He had also discussed his ideas and plans with the representatives of Kerala Granthasala Sangham, Chairman of the District Library Authority of Calicut and many other library activists and important persons of related fields. He also scrutinised the concerned statistical data furnished by the government. Then he worked out the library bill and development plan.

Library Bill of Kerala, 1959

In a conference in which, Education Minister, Director of Public Instruction, Secretary for Education and other concerned officials were present Ranganathan presented the 'Library development plan with a draft library bill for the Kerala State'[9].

It was a comprehensive report in five parts which touched all aspects of the development of a public library system in the State[10]. It consisted of the general principles for the design of a public library system as part one. The second part was the Kerala Public Library Bill. It was based on the earlier bill made for Travancore and the Madras Library Act. But carefully evaluating a decade's working of the Madras Library Act, Ranganathan has rectified its weak points in the bill for Kerala. He has also considered all the later developments throughout the world while preparing this new bill. The system envisaged in the bill was one having a State Central Library for the whole State, a city library for every city having a population of more than 1,00,000 about 250 branch libraries and about 10,000 service stations. The bill contained provisions for State Library Authority the Chairman of which would be Minister for Education. There were provision for State Library Committee, City Library Authority and Rural Library Authority. Provisions were also there for executive committees, sub-committees, branch committees and village library committees with specified duties and powers. There was also provision for collection of library cess by local authorities and for its transmission to the local library authorities concerned within the end of three months after the collection. Third part of the report provided model rules. Fourth part suggested several phases for the implementation of the Act, during which integration of the innumerable small libraries and establishment of viable number of central and branch libraries is to be achieved. An estimate is made of the ultimate and immediate number of professional and semi-professional staff required and their qualifications, salary, scale and status. The last part of the report explained the need for immediate recognition of Trivandrum Public Library, the oldest and largest collection of documents existing at that time as State Central Library in such a way that it will fit in with the system and that its collection will become useful for all the people of Kerala. The pooling together of the resources of Educational Library, Kerala Legislature Library, Secretariat Central Library etc. for the mutual benefit was also suggested[11]. In the plan Ranganathan has included even the syllabus for Bachelors Degree and Certificate Courses in Library Science; which are to train professionals required for the system. Eventhough it was not formally acknowledged the content of BLISC and CLISC courses started in University of Kerala, Public Library and Granthasala Sangham were based on this syllabus. The document also pointed out the limitations of the existing set-up and trend.

In the conference Ranganathan discussed with the Education Minister and other officials all the clauses of the bill and all aspects of the development plan. Mundasseri was highly impressed by Ranganathan's ideas and the bill and the plan received the general approval of the Minister and officials[12]. To make the Bill and the plan available to the public for discussion, before it being moved in the legislature, Government published Ranganathan's Report containing the bill and plan in 1960.

Obstruction by Sangham

The library bill and the development plan met with strong opposition from the Kerala Granthasala Sangham. Sangham and its constituent units denounced the Bill as undemocratic and therefore unacceptable. Another issue was that the bill conceived State Central Library the centre of a solar system around which other libraries would gravitate. Sangham workers were against such streamlined system. What they wanted was totally independent small library units with Sangham as its higher authority which would collect and distribute finance, protect their existence and insist on no standards of service[13]. But Ranganathan's scheme gave no preponderant position to the Sangham or considered its existing system. So Sangham alleged that if the bill became law then government would become the controlling authority and the library system would degenerate into a department of government. What Sangham had in mind was it to be recognized as the supreme authority in the field of library movement in the affairs of which government would not make any direct interference. Top office bearers of the Sangham raised a cry of 'democracy in danger' because they thought, the replacement of the Sangham a democratically organized body; by a government created library authority on the basis of appointment and not by election, would be not only undemocratic but positively anti democratic. The leaders of the Sangham influenced its constituent units; the various Taluk Library Unions to pass resolutions against the bill, copies of which were forwarded to the government by the Sangham[14].

Sangham also submitted to the government a memorandum of its disagreement with government's views and suggestions and demanded fundamental changes in the bill and plan prepared by Ranganathan[15].

Library Bill by Sangham, 1960

Sangham's Executive Committee then authorised one of its patrons Sri Panampally Govinda Menon the former Minister to prepare a Draft Bill as a counter to Ranganathan's Bill. The Bill was ready in 1960. But Menon who had constructive ideas on this subject, and who appreciated Ranganathan's ideas, eventhough tried his best to satisfy some of the Sanghams intentions prepared the Bill in a way in which it will give a scientifically organized and efficient system for public libraries. So Sangham was not satisfied with this bill also. Leading members of the Sangham differed among themselves so widely that they could not come to an agreement on the bill[16]. That was the end of Sangham's own Library Bill.

But Sangham continued its work against the attempts of the Communist Ministry to enact a library legislation. Due to Sangham's strong political affiliations, and its mighty opposition through demonstrations organized in thousands of places throughout the State by its volunteers, and other publicity methods against the bill the government could not proceed with the bill of Ranganathan. Before Mundasseri could seek further advice on the matter the Ministry was dismissed by the Centre.

Attempts by Congress Ministry

Ranganathan again discussed the bill with the next Chief Minister Pattom Thanu Pillai[17]. The Minister personally evaluated the Bill and was in favour of the Bill inspite of the opposition and wide publicity given against it by the Sangham. Knowing that the Bill again came into consideration Sangham expressed its objections to the government and insisted on its having majority representation on the State Library Committee and the Local Library Authorities. Before the Bill could be introduced in the Legislature Sri R. Shankar became Chief Minister. In the meantime the work on the Mysore Library Bill had suggested methods for a more equitable distribution of the library cess than had been provided in the Madras Act and continued in the Kerala Bill. So R. Shankar sought the advisce of Ranganathan about the changes required in the Kerala Library Bill, and sent to him the required financial data and other relevant information. But before Ranganathan could make necessary changes in the bill on the light of these data the President's rule came into force in Kerala.

State Library Service

Though Kerala Library Bill prepared by Ranganathan could not get through in Kerala, other States utilized the revolutionary ideas it contained[18]. This Bill gave more advanced provisions concerning employees of public libraries. Until the Kerala Library Bill was drafted by Ranganathan, there was no concept of a State Library Service. In 1962 Department of Public Libraries in Andhra Pradesh organized a seminar on public libraries. Sri Raghava Reddy a disciple of Ranganathan was then the Director of Public Libraries. Reddy invited Ranganathan to lead the seminar. Ranganathan seized this opportunity to have a public opinion on the Kerala Public Library Bill prepared by him in 1959. He placed it for discussion before the librarians and elected members of the local library authorities who participated in the seminar. They discussed the pros and cons of various provisions of the bill. These discussions no doubt changed the course of future library acts. Mysore Library Act 1965 carried the fruits of this seminar. In it the provision for State Library Service was introduced for the first time in the history of the library movement in India. Librarians working under Local Library Authorities were to be treated as government employees in unmistakable terms. West Bengal Public Library Act has also carried this provision and public library bills pending in various States have made distinct provision for State Library Service. The seminar also ultimately recommended levy of library cess on both property tax and land revenue. The Mysore Act 1965 carried both these provisions. The Mysore Act which was later renamed as Karnataka Public Library Act is almost identical with the Library Bill Ranganathan has prepared for Kerala. It is considered by all experts as the best Library Act now existing in India.

Plan Far-advanced than the Times

When we compare the Kerala Public Library Bill 1959 with the later Bills that came up in Kerala, the legislations that were enacted in other Indian States and in all other regions of the world it will become clear that the Library System that Ranganathan has envisaged in the bill is the most complete and perfect one than those existing anywhere else in the world even in the present day. But like the man behind this idea, the idea was also far-advanced than our times and like in all other periods of history, society cannot understand or accept such ideas.

REFERENCES

1. Kerala, Legislature, Secretariat of -. Kerala Public Library Bill 1971: Background materials. Trivandrum: the author, 1972.
2. Gopinath, M.A. History of library legislation in India. In Ranganathan, S.R., Ed. *Public Library System.* Bangalore: SREL, 1972.
3. Raman Nair, R. Attaniyillattavanum arivu pakaran. Trivandrum: *Kerala Patrika.* 24.11.1986.
4. Gopinath, *Op. cit.,* 2.
5. *Ibid.*
6. Narayana Pillai, C. Dr. S.R. Ranganathan's report. Trivandrum: *Granthalokam,* September, 1960.
7. *Ibid.*
8. Kerala Legislature. *Op. cit.,* 1.
9. Ramanujan Nair, P. *The Library Movement in Kerala.* Trivandrum: Writers Club, 1974.
10. Ranganathan, S.R. *Library Development Plan with a Draft Library Bill for Kerala State.* Trivandrum: Govt. Press, 1960.
11. *Ibid.*
12. Kerala, Legislature. *Op. cit.,* 1.
13. Raman Nair, R. Kerala Granthasala Sangham lakshyam nediyo? Cochin: *Veekshanam,* 12.08.1987.
14. Resolutions passed by various Taluk Library Unions of Kerala Granthasala Sangham published in its *Journal Granthalokam* during October, November and December, 1960.
15. Memorandum submitted to Government by Kerala Granthasala Sangham published in *Granthalokam,* November, 1960.
16. Mani, C.K. Twenty-five years of progress, *Kerala Granthasala Sangham 1945-1970.* In papers of 27th State Conference of the Sangham. Kottayam: KGS, 1972.
17. Kerala, Legislature, *Op. cit.,* 1.
18. Syed Ali Hashmi. Library legislation in India in ILA conference papers, New Delhi, ILA, 1983.

11

DEGENERATION OF THE CONCEPT

History of the library movement in Kerala during the modern phase supports the views of Norris on Library history[1]. The movement was not at all a kind of evolutionary process whereby it has grown better and better. The library system, which the modernising Dewan C.P. Ramaswamy Aiyar and the Communist Ministries headed by the greatest political thinker of our time Sri E.M.S. Namboodiripad have tried to implement with the help of the world renowned expert on the field S.R. Ranganathan, was far advanced than any of such systems existing in India even at present. The Bill framed by Ranganathan, which the Government of Kerala tried to adopt envisaged the pooling of all the information resources of the State and making it available through the system for the benefit of the common people. Even in the West such concept of resource sharing and networking has not reached to that level at that time. This was a magnificent interlude in the history of library movement in Kerala. But before long they became neglected and forgotten. What we see afterwards in Kerala is the degeneration of the concept related to people's library and information system. As viewed by Savage in his theory of occultations the excellent ideas and concepts, after shining upon us for some time have faded again into obscurity[2].

Kerala Public Library Bill, 1969

For almost a decade afterwards there was no noticeable effort on the part of the government in the direction of providing a library legislation. At last in 1969 the coalition government headed by E.M.S. Namboodiripad took up the issue inspite of his bitter experiences of 1960. The Secretary of the Department of Education met Ranganathan to know from him if any improvement in 1959 Bill is required on the light of later developments. Along with the suggestions given by Ranganathan; this time the Government considered the views of the Sangham also because it did not want; as in 1959 to construct afresh a purely scientific system against the will of the Sangham[3]. Government prepared the Kerala Public Library Bill 1969[4]. From all the relevant information government has gathered before preparing the Bill, it understood that accepting the system of Sangham as it is, will hinder the purpose for which a public library system and legislation are intended in the modern days. Even than the Bill was to some extent a conciliation with the motives of the Sangham. It therefore, sought to provide a comprehensive legislation for the recognition of all that is the existing library system in the State, as also for its further development and satisfactory administrative control.

In the proposed legislation the creation of State Library Authority was envisaged with the Minister for Education as ex-officio Chairman, and consisting of three members of the legislature, one member from the syndicate of each university in the State, nine representatives of Sangham, three representatives of District Library Authority by election, an expert in Library Science nominated by the Government, one representative of Kerala Sahitya Academy, Secretary of Education Department, Director of Public Instruction and State Librarian as Ex-officio Secretary[5].

Objections by the Sangham

The Communist Ministry made an attempt to introduce the Bill in the Legislature. But Sangham was not happy with this bill also, because it wanted the government to recognize the necessity for continued working of the Sangham as the central authority of the library system of the State. Further the Sangham felt convinced that the government was not competent to undertake similar work. Sangham explained that in Cochin State the library system under government control was a failure. It also pointed out the ineffectiveness of the functioning of libraries in Malabar under Local Library Authorities. Due to Sangham's opposition and the strong political alliances it could get, the government again failed to enact the bill. Before it could think further the Ministry has to resign.

Now Granthasala Sangham started to exert pressure to enact a legislation which could strengthen its position. In 1970 a member of the Legislature Sri K.G. Kunjukrishna Pillai sought to move a private member's bill known as Kerala Granthasala Bill 1970[6]. But the Bill did not come up for consideration as the assembly met with premature dissolution.

Kerala Public Library Bill, 1971

Due to continued representations by Sangham the then Minister for Education Sri C.H. Mohammed Koya introduced in the Assembly, Kerala Public Libraries Bill 1971. This bill also was intended to give a somewhat efficient system for public libraries on modern lines and was not intended simply to legalize Sangham's views. The Bill was not discussed in the Assembly. But the Bill was printed by the Legislature and copies were distributed among the members. Relevant documents for the study of the Bill was also collected and published by the secretariat of the Kerala Legislative Assembly in 1972 to enable the members to critically evaluate the bill by themselves before further proceedings[7].

The 1971 Bill sought to provide a system for the establishment and maintenance of public libraries and the organization of a comprehensive rural and urban library service in the State. It stipulated that there should be a State Library Authority for the State and District Library Authorities for each District and their composition are sought to be as follows[8]. They will consist of the elected representatives from Members of Legislative Assembly, various cultural organizations like Sangeetha Nataka Academy etc. and the Sangham's representatives nominated by government. The Chairman of the State Library Authority was to be the Minister for Education. The Chairman of the District Library Authority was to be elected from among the members. As regards the provision of the finance the Bill maintained that the fund for the authorities consists of the cess collected by the local bodies at the rate up to 10 per cent of the property tax, grant paid by government equal to the library cess collected, contributions and income from endowments made to the authority for the benefit of the public libraries and any other grant that the central or State government may make, and funds and other amounts collected by the authorities under the rules or by-laws made under the bill. There will be a Director of Libraries with prescribed qualifications who will be the Secretary of the State Library Authority[9]. The Bill provided for the adsorption into the statutory system, all the existing public libraries in the State. There was no provision for separate Library Authorities to look after the City Library systems. There was no provision in the bill for the establishment of a State Central library. These and many other defects and lack of a lot of required provisions makes it clear that the bill was not an improvement over the one prepared by Ranganathan in 1959. Even then the bill accepted some of the modern trends and was not intended to simply give a legal sanction to the system established by Sangham.

Dissatisfaction of the Sangham

So leaders of the Sangham were again dissatisfied with the bill. Their main attack was on the creation of State and District Library Authorities. They voiced their concern at the delegates conference of Sangham in February 1972. Their apprehension was that State Library Authority created by the Bill, would practically be a department of government[10]. The reason for Sangham's opposition again is that if the Bill was enacted Sangham will be pushed to the background; that Sangham will be eclipsed by State Library Authority. The resolutions taken at the Sangham's conference of 1972, for the first time expressed its views and motives on this regard totally and clearly.

Sangham's attempts to Gain Power

The 1972 conference resolved that Sangham must be recognized as a statutory body. In other words it meant that Sangham does not want any other State Library Authority. Sangham wanted itself to be the Authority[11]. The Sangham which is an association registered under Company Law, therefore, should be transformed to a statutory body. Regarding its functions it wanted the transfer of all the social and cultural functions from the Department of Education to the Sangham. About the necessary changes to be brought about in the composition, the Sangham was satisfied with its own administrative set-up. But many participants expressed their views and argued that a scientifically organized system for public libraries has become urgent and important. So in the conference came up the following suggestions. Administrative committee or the governing council of the Sangham shall have two elected representatives of each district instead of three as at present, three government nominees and two nominees of the universities[12]. In order to facilitate efficiency, the Sangham suggested the creation of small executive committee consisting of nine members of the governing body. The Sangham welcomed the appointment of an administrative officer. Government in consultation with the governing body of the Sangham may appoint every three years a financial commission to determine the criterion for the financial aid[13].

To maintain and sustain democratic character of the library movement, and give room for vast development in future; Sangham suggested the creation of a Library Development Council at the State level and district level. The council at the State level should consist of the Minister of Education as its Chairman and as members; Education Secretary, Minister for Local Bodies, Director of Public Instruction, Director of Panchayats, Director of Municipalities, four representatives from State Legislative Assembly, one representative of the University, three representatives of Sangham including its president and secretary, one representative of women's organizations, one or two representatives of the cultural organizations as nominated by government and Secretary of Education as Secretary of the council[14]. Even though these resolutions made by the conference showed acceptance of some progressive ideas by the participants, Sangham failed to proceed on these lines because the leaders were not interested in these ideas. They were interested only in maintaining their authority and the resolutions remained as mere records.

Kerala Granthasala Sangham Bill, 1973

As all successive governments were trying to enact library legislation which could give a good system for library and information service to the people instead of legalizing the Sangham and its system; the leaders of the Sangham thought, now they have to take initiative in immediately preparing a Bill in which Sangham will be the State Library Authority. The 1971 Bill was still active and was being discussed by professional associations and legislators. Sangham feared a chance for its enactment. So Sangham approached Justice V.R. Krishna Iyer to draft a bill which will give legal sanction for the Granthasala Sangham. While he came to Kerala Krishna Iyer discussed Sangham's views with Education Minister and concerned higher officials. But they were not agreeable. Afterwards he prepared a Bill and sent it to Sangham[15]. It is known as Kerala Granthasala Sangham Draft Bill 1973. The bill provided for legalizing Sangham as Library Authority in the State with its existing system as library system from the date of enactment of the Bill and transfer of all libraries and related institutions to the control of the Sangham from that date[16]. Sangham was totally satisfied with the Bill. Immediately after the receipt of the Bill Sangham conducted demonstrations before the Legislative Assembly Building asking the government to disregard the 1971 Bill and enact the Bill prepared by V.R. Krishna Iyer for the Sangham.

Government was not agreeable to give legislative sanction to the obsolete system suggested by Sangham, which all the experts considered to be not fit for organizing library and information service to the people. In 1974 Sri Chakkeri Ahmed Kutty, Minister for Education reintroduced in the Legislature the Kerala Public Libraries Bill 1971 and the House referred it to a select committee[17]. The select committee had various sittings at different centres in Kerala and it collected evidence from the public. Sangham gave wide publicity to the views against the Bill during this period which influenced the evidences negatively. Before the select committee could prepare their report the term of Assembly was over.

Kerala Public Libraries Bill, 1977

In 1977 another Bill was presented to the Assembly by the Minister for Education Sri U.A. Beeran[18]. The Bill has provision for the constitution of a State Library Authority. It will be the highest statutory body responsible for the administration of public library legislation. There was provision for 19 members in the State Library Authority. The Director of Libraries and Education Secretary are ex-officio Chairman and Vice-Chairman respectively. Another ex-officio member was the Director of Public Instruction. Other members are two persons elected from the Kerala Legislative Assembly, three persons from the Bharanasamithi of Kerala Granthasala Sangham, two members elected by the District Library Authority, one person each elected by the Kerala Sahitya Academy, Kerala Lalit Kala Academy, Kerala Sangeetha Nataka Academy, one Library Science expert nominated by Government and one person elected by the Syndicate of each university.

The Bill gives provision for the establishment and maintenance of more than one State Library and deems Trivandrum Public Library only as one of them. The Bill also provides for the District Library Authorities for the purpose of organizing library service at the District level, with sixteen members; representing members of municipal council, panchayat, representation from Sangham, a nominee by District Collector, District Educational Officer, one person from teaching staff of colleges, one headmaster of a high school, and the District Librarian. The Chairman and Vice-Chairman are to be elected from the members of the District Library Authority.

The Bill provided for the collection of a cess from all persons liable to pay property tax at the rate of not more than 10 per cent of the tax. The Government will pay in advance the cess amount to the District

Library Authority. This will be later adjusted in the amount along with property tax. The Government may provide a grant equal to the cess collected, to the District Library Authorities. This along with the cess received, contributions, gifts, income from endowment, and any other grant from Central or State Government will constitute the District Library Fund. Similarly there was provision for State Library Fund also. According to the Bill the State Library Authority or District Library Authority can make bye laws for the achievement of the purposes of the Act. The Bill said that all libraries in each district will stand transferred and vested in the concerned District Library Authorities from a particular date to be fixed by the Government. This will mean that after enactment of this Bill all libraries affiliated to Sangham and all libraries under the local library authorities in the Malabar area will become the libraries under the control and management of the District Library Authorities concerned.

The Bill was referred to the select committee. Select committee collected evidences and a report was presented[19]. But the select committee report could not be considered by the Legislature as the Assembly was again dissolved.

Library Legislation Awareness

Indian Library Association conducted one of its annual conferences at Trivandrum the capital of Kerala. Their major topic of discussion was library legislation. ILA joining with some regional professional organizations drafted and submitted to government a Library Bill which was almost based on Model Bills prepared by Ranganathan and Planning Commission of the Government of India. Many professional associations and cultural organizations of Kerala independent of the Sangham now started to urge the government to enact a library legislation. Leaders of the Sangham utilized all the stages available to them to argue for the need of enacting the Library Bill prepared by them and alleged the government to be inactive and indifferent on this affair and inefficient in its own library development activities. All these raked up the issue of library legislation and kept it a live wire.

Sri T.M. Jacob the Education Minister who was present in many such conferences and cultural meetings in which the topic came for discussion was not able to disregard the matter. In 1985 he introduced a Library Bill. The Bill was prepared after a careful study of all the earlier Kerala Bills and the Library Acts existing in other States. The Bill in its introduction claimed to be one to provide for the establishment maintenance and development of a comprehensive rural and urban library service in the State of Kerala.

Kerala Public Library Bill, 1985

The Kerala Public Library Bill 1985 provided for the constitution and composition of a State, District and Taluk Library Board[20]. State Library Board shall consist of the Minister of the State in charge of Education, as ex-officio Chairman of the Board. Other members were Secretary to Government dealing with libraries, two persons elected by the members of the Kerala Legislative Assembly from among themselves, one person nominated by the Chairman of the Board from among the Heads of the Departments of Library Science of all the universities in the State, the Directors of the Departments of Public Instruction, Libraries, Municipalities and Panchayats and eight persons to be elected by representatives of the affiliated libraries from among themselves[21]. District Library Boards and Taluk Library Boards will be having collector and Tehsildar as Chairman respectively and other members. The bill provided for deeming Trivandrum Public Library the biggest existing public library in the State as a State Library. The State Library Board can establish one or more such State Libraries at places where it may be considered necessary. The Bill also provided for the appointment of a Director of Libraries who shall be the ex-officio Secretary and the Chief Executive Authority of the State Library Board[22]. Regarding the financial provision the Bill provided that government may make every year a grant to the State Library Board a sum which shall not be less than 0.5 per cent and not more than one per cent of the amount allotted for Education in the State Budget. The State Library Board has to maintain a State Library Fund into which grants of State and Central Government and gifts and contributions to State Library Board will be credited. In its totality the 1985 Bill was not at all an improvement over the one prepared by Ranganathan in 1959. Instead of providing for library co-operation and networking which Ranganathan envisaged, this Bill gave powers to State Library Board to establish huge collections at all places where the Board considered it necessary. There was no provision for a State Central Library. Even with all the defects if enacted it would have provided a satisfactory system for public libraries and the services would have become more efficient and reliable[23].

Movement against the Bill

The class related to Kerala Granthasala Sangham in the Bill stated that, with effect on and from the date of which this Bill becomes enacted the Sangham shall be deemed to have been dissolved. All properties and all rights of whatever kind used, enjoyed or possessed by and all interests of whatever kind owned or vested in or held by Sangham shall with effect from the date of enactment of this Bill vest in the State Library Board[24]. It goes without saying that Sangham will never accept such a legislation. Sangham again initiated wide publicity against the bill. Activists and office bearers of Sangham and its constituent units conducted meetings and demonstrations against the bill. Newspapers were flooded with letters to Editor and articles by Sangham's supporters. *Granthalokam* its own journal which reached all its member libraries gave wide publicity to the views against the bill. They alleged the Bill as undemocratic, bureaucratic and useless[25]. Even great personalities in the literary and cultural field like P.T. Bhaskara Panikkar, due to their sentimental attachment to the people's library movement wrote: How an organization formed by the people can be dissolved and for what purpose. The State Library Board provided for in the Bill is surely bureaucratic. It needs to be replaced by Granthasala Sangham. That only will be a democratic decision. For no reasons Granthasala Sangham can be dissolved[26]. Due to all these publicity people began to think that Government has got some ulterior motives in enacting a library legislation. Their attitude became indifferent and somewhat hostile. Because of the opposition of the Sangham and its politics of always influencing the political parties in opposition to government against enacting Library Bills in which it is not interested, the Ministry could not easily proceed with the Bill. The term of the Assembly was also over before the house could further consider the Bill and enact it.

Conciliation by the Communists

In Kerala the communists were always aware of the power of libraries to educate the masses and spread their ideologies and activities into the grass roots of society. None of the other parties were ever considerate about the libraries to that extent. In the capital city they have established a library and research centre of international standard. The Congress which ruled the State for a longer period than the other parties does not have a library of its own[27]. The leaders of most parties with rare exceptions are not known as scholars or for any achievement in educational or professional fields except practical politics. Only the Communist parties happened to be exceptions. They have also a long tradition of the best party library and information system in the State. So it was no wonder that whenever the communists were in power; attempts though not successful were made for library legislation.

In the 1987 elections to the State Legislature, the election manifesto of the Communist party and its allies included, improving the library services in the State on their coming to power as one of the important promises. This may be the first election manifesto of any political party in the country to include library service as an important item. In the election campaign the party activists have explained that the improvement of libraries will be done in accordance with the advice of the Sangham only. In the election campaign's also the volunteers of Sangham were actively engaged in both sides according to their affiliations. So enacting a library legislation has become an important commitment for the party when it came to power. Immediately after its formation, Government started its work on a Library Bill. Remembering all the earlier attempts, instead of entrusting the work to some experts or preparing a bill after studying the acts existing in other States and their working, or following the models suggested by S.R. Ranganathan or Planning Commission of Central Government, the State accepted the views of Sangham and adopted its organizational set-up with very minor alterations. No Library professional organization or expert seems to have associated in the preparation of the Bill. Persons with affiliation to the Sangham and the Ruling Party would have involved in the framing of the Bill for, a member has pointed out in the Assembly during the introduction of the Bill that the State committee of the ruling parties has already decided to pass the legislation in the current session itself[28].

Kerala Public Library Bill, 1989

The new Library Bill was introduced in the State Assembly by the Education Minister Sri K. Chandrasekharan on 3rd February 1989. On the same day it was referred by the House to a subject committee. Many members who were aware of the inefficiency of envisaged system, for giving library service on modern lines wanted the bill to be improved by professional experts. They insisted that the Library Bill should be referred to a Select Committee, so that the professional experts may be able to evaluate and improve it[29]. But that request was not allowed.

Like done by earlier Communist Ministries, the bill was not published and circulated for public discussion.

Instead of dissolving the Sangham as in all earlier bills; this Bill provided for the merging of the Sangham in the Kerala State Library Council from the date of enactment of the Bill[30]. It was in fact not only a mere renaming of the Sangham, but accepting the Sangham as State Library Authority. The constitution and composition of the Kerala State Library Council, provided in the bill was the same as followed for the General Body of the Sangham. Like that the Executive Committee of that council also deferred in name only from Sangham's Barana Samiti. Sangham's District Library Committee came here as District Library Councils and Taluk Library Unions were adopted even without the change in name. Composition of these bodies were the same as followed by Sangham. Elected workers of the socio-cultural movement which was Sangham, dominated the organizational set-up as in Sangham[31]. The Bill very much like the Sangham's views considered this as a system merely meant for organizing socio-cultural and entertainment activities. It was not viewed as a specialized system for the library and information dissemination to the common people and so professionals were given no place in the system. For the first time in its history, Sangham was totally satisfied with the bill and it kept silence. The professional organizations also failed to come up with creative criticism due to the political involvements in the affair, and the too limited time that they got.

Enactment of the Bill, 1989

The subject committee the Chairman of which was also Sri K. Chandrasekharan reported very minor changes only[32]. On February 8, 1989 the Assembly started discussing the bill. There was an eight day long debate at the end of which the Assembly adopted the Kerala Public Library (Kerala Granthasala Sangham) Bill 1989. Even the government has to concede to name the Bill with Sangham's name. But to avoid confusion and objections in getting assistance from the central government and other sources the term Public Library Bill was also included in its name. So the Act also failed to have a standard name. The bill passed by the Legislative Assembly received the assent of the President of India on the 16th May, 1989[33].

No other State in India has got a glorious history of library movement like that of Kerala. Even in the attempts for a library legislation on modern lines Kerala has a long and chequered history.

The fact that many other States in which the library movement is of recent origin, enacted library legislation long before Kerala, that it could not have a library legislation till 1989, that even though its present legislation is one of latest origin it is more defective than all the Library Acts which preceded it, will be rather bewildering to those who are not knowing the undercurrents that existed in Kerala's library movement.

Causes for the Delay and Defects in Legislation

Reasons for the delayed and defective legislation are several. First is the nature of this legislation. Vociferous demands for such social legislations never comes from the part of the people. Most of the social legislations were enforced upon the people by governments for the common good. In such initiative the possibility of losing the support of some strong groups which exploit the existing set-up is always there. Here the Sangham which headed the people's cultural movement and existing system has established itself as a strong socio-cultural organization which can stand with any political party. So no political party or its leader considered modernizing library system as one which could canvass votes.

Inspite of the fact that there was vigorous library movement under the leadership of Sangham it did not have a clear picture of the system needed for library and information services to the people or its required legislation. The Sangham has been clamouring for legislation but it could not produce a draft which can have common consent of its workers and the government. The Sangham which was the dominant organization that was to submit model bills and support the government in enacting a Library Bill torpedoed all the Bills that came up for consideration. The views expressed in its 1972 conference clearly expresses the reasons for Sangham's objections. The demand of the Sangham for library legislation meant not much more than legislating the position of the Sangham as the real authority in matters of libraries in the State and a regular supply of finance by the State Government to the Sangham to manage the affairs of the libraries as well as for its existence. The Sangham wanted minimum interference from the part of the government but maximum financial aid. The Sangham was not ready to accept any proposal for legislation unless the Sangham was recognized as the statutory body and it got the real control of the library system in the State.

The professional associations and experts in the library field who are to pressurise the government for efficient library legislation, who are to prepare and improve the Bills to be considered; were silent and indifferent. This was mostly due to the political involvements in public library movement and the disrespect shown by the movement towards expert systems[34].

REFERENCES

1. Norris, D.M. *History of Cataloguing.* London: Grafton, 1939.
2. Savage, E.A. In his introduction to Thornton, John L. *Chronology of Librarianship,* London: Grafton, 1941.
3. Ramanujan Nair, R. *Library Movement in Kerala.* Trivandrum: Writers Club, 1974.
4. Kerala Government Order No. 25198/43/67 Edn, dtd. 9.7.1969.
5. *Ibid.*
6. Ramanujan Nair. *Op. cit.,* 3.
7. Kerala, Legislature, Secretariat of -. Kerala Public Libraries Bill 1971: Background materials, Trivandrum: the author, 1972.
8. Kerala. Kerala Public Libraries Bill 1971, Trivandrum, Government Press, 1971.
9. *Ibid.*
10. Ramanujan Nair. *Op. cit.,* 3.
11. Raman Nair, R. Kerala Granthasala Sangham Lakshyam Nediyo? Cochin: *Veekshanam,* 12.8.1987.
12. Mani, C.K. Twenty-five years of progress: Kerala Granthasala Sangham 1945-1970. In papers of 27th State Conference of Sangham. Kottayam: Sangham, 1972.
13. *Ibid.*
14. *Ibid.*
15. Panikkar, P.N., Ed. Keralathile Granthasala Prasthanam, Trivandrum: *Steps,* 1982.
16. *Ibid.*
17. Kerala, Legislature, Secretariat of-. Kerala Public Libraries Bill 1985: Background materials. Trivandrum: the author, 1986.
18. Kerala. Kerala Public Libraries Bill 1977. Trivandrum: Government Press, 1977.
19. Kerala, Legislature, Public Libraries Bill, Select Committee on, Chairman: Mohammed Koya, C.H. Report. Trivandrum: Government Press, 1977.
20. Kerala. Kerala Public Library Bill 1985. Trivandrum: Government Press, 1985.
21. *Ibid.*
22. *Ibid.*
23. Raman Nair, R. Granthasala Niyamam: Samuhya Vidhya-Bhyasathinte Adittara. Cochin: *Veekshanam,* 22.11.86.
24. Kerala. *Op. cit.,* 20.
25. Surendran, S.K. Granthasala Samkamillatta Granthasala Bill venda. *Kerala Kaumidhi,* 12.12.1985.

26. Bhaskara Panikkar, P.T. Granthasala Niyamam Inganeyo? *Kerala Kaumidhi,* 3.10.1985.
27. Ramanujan Nair. *Op. cit.,* 3.
28. Public Libraries Bill referred to Subject Committee. Cochin: *Indian Express,* 4.2.1989.
29. *Ibid.*
30. Kerala. Kerala Public Library (Kerala Granthasala Sangham) Bill 1989. Trivandrum: Govt. Press, 1989.
31. Deep roots of library movement. Cochin: *Hindu,* 24.2.1989.
32. Kerala, Legislature, Public Library Bill, Subject Committee on, Chairman: Chandrasekharan, K. Report. Trivandrum: Government Press, 1989.
33. Kerala Government order No. 1951/Leg. C1/89/Law. Dated 18th May, 1989.
34. Raman Nair. *Op. cit.,* 11.

12

PRINCIPLES OF LIBRARY LEGISLATION

Legal provisions related the collection, preservation and distribution of recorded information existed from very ancient times. Instrument of Legislation for the establishment of government or public libraries, and for offering services like making available for consultation or for home reading; manuscripts and other documents have been existing throughout the period of history. When printing was introduced in South India by the missionaries, reading materials started to increase. With that the activity of developing libraries through edicts and legislation gained momentum.

One of the first legislative enactment in the New World was in 1696; when the Maryland Assembly passed several laws to ensure establishment and maintenance of libraries. But the legislation which influenced all later ones throughout the world was British Public Library Act of 1850. The two basic principles that it set out were: first that public libraries in a community should be free from dependence on private gifts, subscriptions or charitable donations; second, that they should be free to include whatever available materials were needed by readers, and therefore that they should not be controlled in such choices either by political or by religious influences[1].

In 1877 when the first International Conference of Librarians was held in London, the Library Association of United Kingdom was formed and among its main objectives we find the deliberation to secure better legislation and the improvement of administration[2]. In the following years we find an interesting history of the development of concepts behind public library legislation.

Systems Concept

Historically speaking all library legislations throughout the world envisaged libraries as independent single units under a Government department. The revolutionary concept of a library system, as distinct from unitary libraries, and legislation for such system; came into existence with the presentation of the Model Library Act by S.R. Ranganathan in the conference at Banaras. This concept emphasises that public libraries at different levels viz. State, city, district along with branches or service units should be so interlinked as to form part of a system or network. Such a public library system can be compared with a large irrigation system. It needs a hand-work with a costly dam and a large number of distributories and sub-distributories through which water can reach every bit of land. The traditional independent libraries on the other hand, resemble more the wells and tanks which have served mankind for ages, but they have limited and dwindling use in modern times. This new concept of system thus offers infinite possibilities due to the following factors.[3]

* It is a co-operative and organic structure in which every unit, however small, is rich as the whole system;
* It has larger funds which allow for a balanced and even-development of public library service over large areas irrespective of local variations or imbalances in financial support;
* It is comparatively more economical; and
* It can provide library services more efficiently and effectively because it can permit introduction of library services based on modern concepts of services and approved standards.

UNESCO has accepted the principles for library legislation enunciated by Ranganathan; in its Public Library Manifesto declared in 1949 revised by IFLA in 1972[4]. The manifesto declares that as a living force for education, culture and information, the public library should be established under the clear mandate of law, so framed as to ensure nationwide provision of public library service. Organized co-operation between libraries is essential so that total national resources should be fully used and at the service of the reader[5].

National Network

Ranganathan in his Library Development plan published in 1950 by the university of Delhi again stressed that public library development should be planned as library systems rather than on unitary basis[6]. In it he laid much emphasis on the setting up of library services in a well-planned and organized manner in each State and the country as a whole so as not to repeat the mistake of the countries which have gradually made much progress on library development.

The First International Seminar organised by UNESCO on public libraries has accepted this principle by stating that library legislation should provide for the inter-lending of books between libraries so that the book resources of the whole territory shall be available to all[7]. In United States the importance of the systems concept in planning public library services and in enacting library laws has been specifically emphasised in the standards for public library system published in 1967. The standards contained the concept that every individual has a right to benefit from the record of what is known whether he lives in a big city, a suburban community, a small town, an un-incorporated area or a rural district and the structure of such service should provide a flexible, operative library network effectively linking the libraries of the State and Nation[8]. Thus a system would provide accessibility of service through branches, co-operating libraries, and book mobile shops and would plan a pool of resources and services in depth and variety, used in common by all the outlets.

Resource Sharing

Today the concept of legislation for library system is not limited to public libraries. When S.R. Ranganathan suggested in 1959 in his Library Development plan for Kerala, the pooling of the resources of Legislature library, Government Secretariat Library and some other big specialised collections, to make them available to the people through public library system, even library professionals were not prepared to accept the idea. But now UNESCO and several other international agencies such as IFLA and FIO have accepted the concept of National Information Systems (NATIS) which pools the information resources of all types of libraries so that they become available to all the people in a country. An important objective of NATIS is that; the functions of all documentation, library and archives services should be coordinated through a central body to form the NATIS, so as to ensure the optimum use of available resources and maximum contribution to the cultural, social and economic development of each nation.

Systems Legislation

With the growing emphasis on the development of large library and information systems, following the realization that local library services needed to be supplemented with resources from outside the local area, there has been a steady interest in library legislation concerning regional library systems, metropolitan urban library systems, State Library systems and multi-State systems. Various countries have enacted legislation creating nation wide public library systems. In many countries where library legislation existed, the legislators have revised and altered those legislations in accordance with this modern concept.

Public library legislation is designed to set out a particular policy as well as the means to be used to implement it. The fundamental steps in the preparation of such legislation are: to define the aim of the legislation; to reach an agreement concerning the terms in which legislative policy can be expressed; and finally to formulate the texts setting out the policy question[9].

Evaluation and Revision

State and National governments have to answer the following questions[10]: Is the present legislation suitable and does it facilitate future developments and cooperative endeavours? Does it provide the supervising agency with an authority commensurate with the needs of libraries? Does it set throughout the country a uniform standard of library service? Does it stipulate in clear terms the amount of financial support to be granted? If the answer to some or all of these questions is no, then there is a need to revise the existing legislation. Some of the methods which many countries have successfully used to upgrade the quality of their public library legislation are the following[11]:

* Carrying out studies of provisions in neighbouring countries' legislations which already make provisions for the attainment of some or all, of agreed public library objectives;
* Introducing the need for public library improvement along with other social and educational changes, into the political platforms of local regional or national parties;
* Establishing demonstration projects to show what could be

achieved on a wider scale if relevant legislative provision existed for all parts of the region or nation; and

* Holding local seminars and workshops with the participation of the public in order to bring the voters' pressure to bear on the elected representatives in government.

These can be undertaken through the combined efforts of library leaders, librarians and voluntary citizen groups.

Guidelines for Library Legislation

Considering the complexity, diversity and range of individual, national, public library legislations, UNESCO has produced general guidelines which might be used to introduce new legislation in countries that might need it. The document prepared for UNESCO by Frank M. Gardner, 'Public Library Legislation a Comparative Study' lays down a series of principles for the formulation of public library law which have been used with success by many framers of legislation. The general necessary legal provisions emphasised in Gardner's study were the following[12]:

Areas of Basic Concern

* Use of the libraries should be free and open to all.
* The materials to be provided and the services to be given should be specified.
* The administrative unit should be responsible for the entire territory of the area served, whether national regional or local.
* There should be an independent body charged with the duty of advising on the implementation of the legislation. This should come under the national government department named to be responsible for public library development.

Powers of the Central Authority

* It should be able to make services compulsory.
* It should have powers of inspection, and should set standards, and have a staff to carry out its supervisory functions.
* It should make regulations on all matters affecting public libraries.
* It should enable local authorities to make regulations, and should

provide guidance and assist in their elaboration.

Financial Provisions

* The Central Government should provide financial assistance by way of grants, both for regular and for specific and experimental purposes.
* The local authority should be empowered to levy relevant taxes.
* The library authority should have the power to raise money for capital expenditures.

Nationwide Library Networks

* There should be provision for a mechanism for co-operation and interlending.
* There should be provision for the joint running of services, in co-operation with other agencies.
* Library services should be provided to various agencies, community centres, hospitals etc.
* Institutionally owned libraries should be able to be integrated into the general public library system.

Requirements in Indian Situations

In the development of large public library systems as that is required in India, according to H.C. Campbell special attention should be made to the following matters: the powers of the central authority; provision for co-operation; services provided by a national library; and the special situation of federal countries[13].

UNESCO Inter-governmental Conference on the planning of national documentation, library and archive infrastructures, placed major emphasis on the need for adequate national public library legislation. Objective adopted by the conference for setting up national information systems dealt with the establishment of necessary national legislative framework designed to ensure the participation of the central government and the co-ordination of national efforts.

The document on legislative framework for the implementation of NATIS gives a very good approach that can be taken by any national government towards achieving national coverage or public library service[14]. The document states that it is however unrealistic to legislate for the compulsory provision of library services without taking into account the current state of library development and the steps which have to be taken before a service of the required standard can be provided. In the absence of the self-regulating mechanism of permissive legislation, a means has to be found to enable a service to be progressively extended, from existing or newly established bases, across the whole country. This process must be flexible, so that progress can be adjusted in the light of the experience or changing factors. Time-tables and deadlines embodied in legislation are like smouldering time bombs which eventually have to be diffused by amending legislation. One answer lies in placing responsibility for the development of the library service in the hands of a Minister accountable to Parliament or Legislature and empowering him to make orders extending compulsory provision to administrative units as development makes this possible.

National Level Legislation

In countries with strong tradition of local autonomy there have been attempts to provide for a form of Central Governmental authority that allows for local autonomy as well as for various forms of national planning, supervision and co-ordination. One example of legislative success in this area is that of United Kingdom where a revised Public Library Act was passed in 1964 complimented by another Act in 1972 which set up British Library Board and gave that body the responsibility of working with municipal public library systems and other types of libraries to promote better service[15]. Among its various responsibilities the British Library Board is empowered to develop a wide range of central services, link them with local authorities, and carry out and sponsor research in public library development and methods of work.

For library legislation making adequate provision for library co-operation; Czechoslovakia and Hungary are two excellent examples[16]. In these countries whose respective national goals in the area of library development are to offer the general public access to every type of reading materials, the national authorities have created a comprehensive system of school, community, trade union and other libraries and provided adequate financial support. These legislation provide for (a) the establishment of a unified system of libraries—the main objective of this section of the law is to indicate the mission and function of libraries in a socialist society and to declare that all libraries, whether school, trade-union, public, special, university, etc., are important factors in socialistic education; and (b) the formal devaluation of responsibility for resource-sharing and library co-operation which is a basic objective of all library legislation in socialist countries.

The library legislation should also clearly define the role of National and State Central Library in national information system. The National Library should be given leadership role in NATIS.

State Level Legislation

In most federal countries, the separate authorities of the constituent parts of the federation must be considered. For instance, the present Australian legislation has established a State Library Authority in each federal State to assist local government authorities, manage the State library and provide other library and information services to the public. However no State legislation requires some authority to provide library and information service to its residents.

The most important consideration in the framing of a legislation is the nature of the State itself and the place that legislation takes in its structure. In social legislation like the one meant for the establishment of public library systems, account must be taken of the various aspects such as the nature of authority by which national government passes on its authorities, the basis of taxation at local and national level, and in a federal State like India, the constitutional rights of the established organisms within the State. A comparative study of the library legislation in certain countries of the world vindicates that while legislation differs from country to country similar problems do eventually tend to produce similar solutions, and similarity in governmental structure also tend to impose a pattern.

REFERENCES

1. Campbell, H.C. *Developing Public Library Systems and Services.* Paris: UNESCO, 1983.
2. Prakash Vegad, P. Public library legislation: Its role in developing library systems. In Biswas, S.C. *Public Library Development and Perspectives.* New Delhi: ILA, 1985.
3. Mangala, PB. Library legislation in India. In Rout, R.K. *Library Legislation in India: Problems and Prospects.* New Delhi: Reliance 1986.
4. UNESCO. UNESCO *Public Library Manifesto.* Paris: UNESCO, 1972.
5. *Ibid.*
6. Ranganathan, S.R. Library development plan: thirty year programme for India with draft bills for the union and the constituent States. New Delhi: University of Delhi.
7. UNESCO, Development of public libraries, Seminar on Ibadan, In UNESCO Manuals for libraries. Paris: UNESCO, 1954.

8. American Library Association, Public Library Association, Standards Committee. Minimum standards for public library system. Chicago: ALA, 1966.
9. Campbell. *Op cit,* 1.
10. *Ibid.*
11. *Ibid.*
12. Gardner, Frank M. *Public Library Legislation: A Comparative Study.* Revised and updated by H.C. Campbell. Paris: UNESCO, 1978.
13. Campbell. *Op. cit.,* 1.
14. UNESCO. *Establishing a Legislative Framework for the Implementation of NATIS.* Paris: UNESCO, 1977.
15. Hook, HT. The organization of library systems and the example of Britain. In Canadian Library Association's conference proceedings. Ottawa: CL4, 1974.
16. Campbell. *Op. cit.,* 1.

13

LIBRARY ACT : AN EVALUATION

The growth of knowledge and the direct relation of information to developments in all walks of human life emphasises the need to give more priority to the planning of systems which give library and information services to the people. Such systems can only be planned at national level, if the total information and document resources of the nation is to be pooled together in a federal country like India, and shared between the constituent States to make available to all the users who require it in an equal and unbiased way at optimal cost. Such systems should be founded upon sound legislation, lest the objectives will ever remain unattainable.

The pressure of the information need of the society has become so imperative that many of the national and international library organizations have started to stress the urgent need for national library systems working together and sharing their services and materials at international level to provide better services to the people. Better can be defined here in quantitative as well as qualitative terms. Such national level and international level networking and resource sharing between library systems make possible service at lower cost, access to more materials, more rapid availability of materials and convenience of access[1].

Need for Uniform Pattern

For providing improved library services more economically by pooling resources and sharing resources, a library and information system should be planned as a national system with a national level legislation supporting that system. To enable such a national level system all the

States which are component units in a federal structure like India should have a uniform pattern of library and information systems, so that these components can be organized into a coherent whole. It requires a uniform pattern for State library legislations also. So Union should enact a national library and information service Act, which shall prescribe a model library act for the States. The Union Government should also prescribe a time limit within which the States are to develop library systems according to the pattern suggested by the union government.

With these motives in mind Dr. S.R. Ranganathan has framed the first model public libraries act in 1930 which he placed for discussion at the Educational Conference at Banaras. Before framing the act, this internationally reputed library scientist has travelled through most countries of the world where library legislation existed and has evaluated them and in many countries his ideas helped them to improve the systems. So the Model Act of 1930 was an improved and advanced one than any of the existing acts. In his Library Development Plan which he submitted in 1947 to Government of India he has also included a union library bill and a revised State library bill which envisaged the national public library and information system according to the most modern principles[2]. Another model library act was drafted in 1963 by a committee under the chairmanship of Shri. D.M. Sen on behalf of the Ministry of Education, Government of India. In 1966 the Library Legislation Sub-Committee of the Planning Commission also prepared a model bill.

Measuring Rod

The library acts that came into existence in Madras, Hyderabad, Andhra, Karnataka and Maharashtra totally or partially accepted the ideas of Ranganathan as reflected in his Model Acts and bills. These States became the laboratories where the ideas evolved by Ranganathan were experimented and observed. In the light of the observations made in the States where library acts came into force and also considering the suggestions contained in the other model bills, Ranganathan has improved his model act by rectifying the clauses found to be defective in working and by adding new provisions that seemed essential. This model libraries act was published in 1972[3]. This is the latest and most advanced Model Act. Eight States out of the 25 States and 7 union territories have enacted library legislation. They are Madras 1948, Andhra 1960, Karnataka 1965, Maharashtra 1967, West Bengal 1979,

Manipur 1985, Kerala 1989 and Haryana 1989. But none of them are considered totally perfect or efficient.

So in this comparative analysis of the essential aspects of Kerala Public Library (Kerala Granthasala Sangham) Act, 1989; the Model Public Library Act 1972 of Dr. S.R. Ranganathan, is taken as the measuring rod or ideal situation with which the State Act is compared. Whenever some notable additional provisions or improvements are found in other existing Acts the same is discussed at the concerned context. The Kerala Act and Ranganathan's Model Act of 1972 will be referred herein after as KPLA and Model Act respectively.

Preamble

The preamble of a Library Act should summarise and state the aims and objectives of that Library Act. Even though the preamble of KPLA went on to explain the existing situations and the intentions with which the Act was initiated in an elaborate and vague form, it has given what is to be in preamble just before thc preamble in precise and clear words as a long title of the Act. This summary or long title of the Act which we have to consider as preamble contains the basic concept of modern public library service which the actual preamble failed to state and the KPLA in its totality failed to support.

Like the Model Act, this summary provides for the establishment and maintenance of a system of public libraries and for the comprehensive development and organization of all kinds of library and information services required for the people. The long title that follows the title of the Act in KPLA states, it is: an Act to consolidate and unify the library laws in the State and to provide for the reorganization of the entire library system in the State of Kerala with a view to the development and maintenance of a comprehensive rural and urban library service and for matters connected therewith or incidental thereto[4].

Ranganathan has laid clear emphasis on legislation for public library service and for the organization of a comprehensive library system. But all other acts except KPLA provides for establishment and maintenance of public libraries only. They all cling to the obsolete concept of treating public libraries as independent units in their collection and services. So in this statement of the purpose of the Act, KPLA has accepted the most modern concept of public library legislation and the statement is a distinct improvement over those in all other existing State Acts.

State Library Authority

The concept of the State Library Authority (SLA) underwent an evolution from State Library Committee to Minister of Education or Libraries; everywhere in the world. The Model Act recommends that for the purpose of promoting and organizing a library system in the State the Minister for Education shall be the SLA[5].

It shall be the duty of the SLA to provide; for an adequate library and information service in the State and, for the progressive development of the institutions devoted to the purpose and to secure the effective execution by Local Library Authorities (LLA) of the national policy for providing adequate library service to the people in every locality.

In the existing State Acts only Karnataka Public Library Act, 1965 provides and clearly names SLA. Section 3 of the Act provides for the constitution and composition of the SLA[6]. SLA shall be a body corporate having perpetual succession and a common seal with power, to acquire, hold and dispose of property and to contract and may be the same time sue and be sued. It consists of twenty members from the fields concerned with information creation, organization and services, with Minister for Education who shall ex-officio be the president and State Librarian who shall ex-officio be the Secretary of SLA.

But it is desirable to make only one person, instead of a corporate body to be the supreme authority for providing this very important service, for that gives a unified command from administrative points of view. And this person should not be any person less than the Minister for Education, because he is directly responsible to the legislature and his term of office being limited to a period of five years he is ultimately responsible to the people. According to Hewit who made a study of the library legislation in India; it will be observed that two kinds of supreme authority are favoured in existing legislation and in the drafts of the model bills framed in India. One is a body of persons i.e. State Library Council or Committee and second is a Minister of State. He suggests the second as the better of the two, mainly because a Minister is responsible to his legislature and through it to the electors and may be called to account therein. A body of persons eventhough a Minister may be President or Chairman thereof is not so easily questioned. In any case; so important an activity as the provision for public library and information service to the people fully justifies direct representation in State Legislature[7].

So all the studies on library legislation and the evaluation of existing legislation throughout the world and especially in third world countries; like that of Gardner's study comes to the conclusion that providing up of a body or a person as SLA and clearly naming and defining its powers and functions is certainly essential for the successful working of library Acts. But KPLA is very vague in this aspect and it fails to name a person or body as SLA.

State Library Committee

The Model Act provides for a State Library Committee (SLC) for the purpose of advising the SLA on all matters arising under the Act. All existing State Acts and Model Bills enacted or drafted in India provide for appointment of such a Committee or Council[8]. KPLA names it as Kerala State Library Council. All Acts of the States except Kerala's have prescribed its membership on somewhat similar lines. All Acts provides that this body will be headed by Minister for Education. Despite differences in nomenclature and composition the function of this committee or council envisaged everywhere is basically the same i.e. to advise the SLA or State Government in all matters arising out of the Act.

Kerala State Library Council (KSLC)

A careful analysis of the Kerala State Library Council (KSLC) in comparison with the SLC as provided in the Model Act or other State Acts will reveal that it is not a council or committee of advisory nature as SLCs are. KSLC is an SLC and at the same time an SLA by itself. Naming it as a council is a difference in terminology only. Instead of appointing a Minister as SLA as in Mysore it appoints a body as SLA. But the Act fails to name it as SLA. The duties powers and functions assigned to KSLC is inclusive of all those assigned to SLA and SLC in Model Act. Subsection 1 of Section 3 of KPLA dealing with the constitution and composition of KSLC states[9]: KSLC shall be a body corporate having perpetual succession and a common seal with power, to acquire hold and dispose of property, both movable and immovable and to enter into contracts and shall by its name sue and be sued. This is an adaptation of the class related to Karnataka State Library Authority in Karnataka Act[10]. No other Act including Model Act has so clearly defined the nature of this body and assigned so much powers as this like the Acts of Kerala and Karnataka.

The powers and functions assigned to KSLC includes both the advisory functions of the committees and councils provided by Model

Act and other Acts and the duties assigned to SLA by Model Act and Karnataka Act. Subsections of Section 8 of KPLA provides that the KSLC may[11]:

* advise the government on all matters connected with the administration of this Act and . . . the overall library policy of the State.
* co-ordinate the working of the District Library Councils and Taluk Library Unions and . . . supervise and direct all matters relating to library service in the State.
* establish one or more State Libraries . . . at such place or places in the State as may be considered necessary.
* appoint and control such officers and servants as may be necessary for the efficient performance of its duties and functions under this Act and the rules made thereunder.
* give to the District Library Councils and Taluk Library unions directions in the performance of their functions under this Act and . . . they shall not in the discharge of their functions under this Act depart from directions given by the KSLC.

While we consider these classes and compare them with the parallel sections of the Model Act or other Acts it becomes clear that the classes which assigns the duties, powers and functions of KSLC is a distinct improvement from all others. KPLA has identified most of the functions and duties expected from such a body and very clearly assigned them to it without giving place for doubt and vagueness.

Composition of KSLC

If KSLC is to become able to fulfil such duties and functions expected from it, the composition of the body should be done accordingly. Membership of such a body should include persons who have contributed to the growth of knowledge, who have evolved or developed methods and techniques for collecting organizing and disseminating information and who have wide experience in related fields of activity[12]. It is not the method of representation but the quality of representation that will make possible the efficient functioning of the system.

The sections which prescribe the membership of SLA in Karnataka Act and SLC in Model Act and other State Acts prescribe their membership incorporating sufficient professional involvement. Prof. P.B. Mangala in his study of library legislation opines that SLC should be a body having representatives from various institutions, organizations, government etc. interested in and connected with the growth and development of library and information services in the State[13].

The Model Act and also the opinion of experts and recommendations of committees set for studying library legislation agrees that such a body like SLC should include among its members; the Minister for Libraries if there is one, otherwise Minister for Education, then Minister in charge of Local Self Government, Director of Libraries, State Librarian, sufficient number of representatives from State Legislative Assembly by election from among themselves, Secretary to Government for Education, representatives elected from Local library Authorities by rotation to limit size of the body, representatives of associations of library profession and experts with specialization in library and information services and representatives of Universities of the State. It would be essential that the Minister in charge of libraries should act as ex-officio chairman and the Director of Public Libraries or State Librarian should act as ex-officio Secretary of the committee.

The rationale behind such a composition of this body is that it is a body which is to advise the government and discuss continuously on a most important responsibility of the government, that is organization and dissemination of information required by the society. But disregarding all these principles KPLA provides for constituting a body of members who were not suitable to undertake this work. The subsection 2 of Section 3 related to the composition of the KSLC in KPLA provides that the KSLC shall consist of one member each from Taluks, elected by the general body of the District Library councils, and five members of whom one shall be a librarian, another a person belonging to the scheduled caste or scheduled tribe and another a woman nominated by the government[14].

Library and information service is an intellectual service. It goes without saying that this body as provided in KPLA will not be able to fulfil satisfactorily the purpose for which it is intended. In these days of information explosion and flooding of vast and varied types of books and other printed materials that originates every minute, without a wide familiarity of all spheres of knowledge and expertise in handling their information in most effective way at minimum cost the body which heads such a system will be having a mere formal and meaningless existence. As we have seen in Section 8 of KPLA the most important function of KSLC is to advise the government; on all matters connected with the administration of this Act and overall library policy of the State. It is not clear how this committee will be competent to render such expert technical advice when it has only non experts as members, who has come through election without expertise or knowledge about information work and without even any educational qualification. Library and information service to the people if provided efficiently will require expert advice everyday on many matters. The KSLC's inability to provide such expert advice will make government's efforts futile and to overcome this, government will be forced to create a continuous chain of Advisory Committees which is also not very practicable.

While no hard and fast rule can be laid down about the size of this body it is generally felt that it should not have more than twenty members. But membership of this body as per KPLA which is to be constituted according to sub-section 2 of Section 3 which we have already referred will swell upto 67, for Kerala has got 62 Taluks. But the KSLC may remain a supreme body in name only for real powers of the council have been passed over to a smaller body which is the Executive Committee[15]. But it also becomes an unwieldy body with membership of 25 persons. Thus KSLC has accumulated into itself all the defects existing in SLAs and SLCs into one body. This Executive Committee is a new addition in our library acts. But the findings of Ashoka Mehta Committee and various committees appointed by many State Governments to study Panchayat Raj Institutions advice us against such an elected body like KSLC for fulfilling important functions like library and information service to the people.

Instead of adopting the constitution and composition of SLA and SLC provided by the Model Act or followed by the other State Acts KPLA gave legal sanction to the organizational set-up of an association that was already existing in Kerala, that is Kerala Granthasala Sangham. The constitution and composition of KSLC and its Executive Committee is the same followed by Sangham for its general body and Bharanasamithi. In all other provisions KPLA follows the same pattern of Sangham with some minor alterations. For more than half a century Sangham was pressurising the Government to give legal sanction to Sangham to be the SLA and to accept its system as it is as State's Library System[16]. But experts have continuously pointed out during this period the futility of such a system for library and information service. But Sangham during the last four decades objected government's all attempts to enact a modern library system legislation and at last came out successful in legalizing its own system. But this in fact totally prevents the State from having an advanced library legislation and developing library and information services in conformity with the requirements of the time.

Local Library Authority

Library and information service is to be rendered locally by thousands of service points spread throughout the State. The State as a whole in view of its large size is not suitable for being considered as a single unit for organizing these services. So it becomes essential to organize this service system on a decentralized pattern. The units of responsibility at different levels and their nature, functions and relation with other levels should be clearly specified in the Act. In the Model Act Ranganathan recommended two types of Local Library Authorities; District Library Authority in a District and City Library Authority in a city.

The KPLA improves the scope of decentralization of services; providing a three tier system that is after State level subsystems at District and Taluk levels parallel to Government's administrative mechanism. The District Library Councils (DLC) and Taluk Library Unions (TLU) are miniature forms of KSLC. Their constitution, composition, powers and functions are all the same as KSLC; limited within the geographical area of its coverage. DLC and TLU shall elect their Executive Committee which will elect the office bearers very much like in KSLC. All the defects of KSLC are reflected in these bodies also. The Act does not provide for City Library Authorities. It is the duty of the Taluk union to organize and administer the library and information service to the people living in Cities and villages.

Department of Public Libraries

It is generally emphasised that in order to develop a system of public libraries in a State or country on proper lines, it is essential that a separate department of public libraries be created at par with the department of education and that the former should not be a part of the latter or any other department[17]. The Acts of Andhra, Maharashtra, West Bengal and Karnataka prescribe for the creation of separate Department of Public Libraries[18].

Director of Public Libraries

Most of the recommendations related to public library system legislation emphasises that the department of Public Libraries should be headed by a Director of Public Libraries (DPL), whose rank must be equivalent to that of Director of Education. He must be a person with qualification and experience in Library and Information Science. Emphasis on his being a professional is laid because it is he to whom the whole public library system in the State would look for guidance and inspiration and his professional outlook would normally be of great help to the development of the system on desired lines.

The first public library act in this country; the Madras Act 1948, provided for the appointment of DPL. Andhra, Maharashtra and West Bengal also prescribes for the creation of DPL. In Madras and Andhra the Director of Public Instruction is made the ex-officio Director of Public Libraries also. The disadvantages of such an administrative set-up are quite obvious. The Department of Public Libraries becomes an additional burden to the Director of Public Instruction. This new department will be looked upon as an uninvited guest. A.R. Hewit has rightly pointed out that many of the duties of Director of Public Libraries would require technical knowledge and skill in librarianship. So only professional experts can undertake this responsibility efficiently.

State Librarian

All the Acts except KPLA which is not providing for these offices, combines the responsibilities of (i) developing and managing the State Central Library as well as (ii) superintending and directing all matters related to the State library system in a single person called State Librarian or DPL. The Model Act also recommends this pattern. But the Sinha committee report suggested the creation of two separate posts for this purpose when it says "The DPL may have the overall responsibility to organize develop and supervise the public library system as Head of the Department of Public Libraries. The State Central Librarian should have the responsibility to manage, supervise and develop State Central Library and should be the Chief Technical Advisor of the DPL, with no responsibility for the administration of the service in the State. This responsibility should be entirely that of DPL. But in KPLA there is no provision for appointing a Director of Libraries or State Librarian. While the class by class discussion of the Bill was going on in Kerala Legislative Assembly, Mr. V.M. Sudheeran; member presented an amendment to add a new clause in the Act providing for appointment of a Director of Libraries[19]. But was not considered.

Administration

For the administration of public libraries all the State Acts have created a department or directorate of public libraries. It is put under the charge of Director of Libraries or State Librarian who is to be the ex-officio Secretary of SLA. The functions of these posts as prescribed by all Acts including the Model Act are: to supervise and direct all matters relating to public libraries, to direct and control the working of LLAs, submit reports to Government and deal with schemes and plans relating to libraries. Many of the highly technical and specialized works of State Central Library also is to be supervised by them. So it is clear that these posts which are carrying heavy responsibility concerning various matters—financial, advisory, administrative, technical, supervisory and so on—under the Act would require technical knowledge and skill in library and information service. So the Secretary or High Officer of this body should be a whole time officer having the prescribed qualifications to practice the library profession.

Disregarding all the above facts KPLA assign all the duties and powers to a Secretary elected by members of the Executive Committee of KSLC. Sub-section 5 of Section 3 of KPLA provides that the elected members of the Executive Committee shall elect a President, Vice-President, Secretary and Joint Secretary from among themselves to be the President, Vice-President, Secretary and Joint Secretary respectively of the State Library Council and of the Executive Committee[20]. Their term of office will be for three years. KPLA assigns to the Secretary of KSLC the duties and powers which other State Acts assign to State Librarian or Director of Libraries. Sub-section 1 of Section 9 states that the Secretary of the State Library Council shall be Chief Executive Authority of KSLC.

The nature of the office of Secretary of KSLC requires professional knowledge and experience as well as continuity of office for the successful operation of the Act. So it is inevitable that this provision for an elected secretary will prevent KPLA from fulfilling the objectives for which a modern library legislation should exist. This serious defect of the Act has been pointed out by many members during the discussion of the bill. Dr. M. Kuttappan has brought to the notice of the Assembly that such an important system like the one for library and information service requires qualified government officials as their Secretaries at State, District and Taluk levels[21]. The period of an elected non official member may be over by three years and if he misappropriates government fund allotted for library development it will not be possible for the government to take action on him[22]. Sri Ishac Kurikkal suggested an amendment to the Bill to provide that the Secretary of the SLC shall be appointed by the Government on the advice of the Kerala Public Service Commission[23]. Another member Sri Kodiyeri Balakrishnan opined that the Secretary of KSLC should be appointed by Government and the Act should specify the qualifications and method of appointment for this post[24]. Sri Ramesh Chennithala presented an amendment to add the following sub-clause in KPLA namely: the Secretary shall be a person not below the rank of a Joint Secretary to Government to be appointed by Government from among persons qualified and competent to hold such post[25]. But all these suggestions were rejected and the accepted principles were disregarded to maintain a democratic system for constituting the SLA.

State Central Library (SCL)

The existing State legislations and the Model Act provide for a State Central Library (SCL) as an integral part of the Public Library Service[26]. The SCL is normally the copy right collection. It should collect as far as its resources allow, expensive work and literature published abroad, material for which the local public library would have little need and could not afford. All the countries of the world possessing adequate library systems, have national library systems and all have national central library as distinct from the other libraries in the system, but is accessible to all through any library of the system. The same role of National Central Library to the national system is to be fulfilled by SCL to the State system. Usually the library legislations designate the biggest collection available in the State as SCL and makes its resources and services available to the system. Even though various Acts and the Model Act give different names to SCL like State Service Library, etc. in a public library system only one such library will be maintained and its resources will be shared by all participating units. Maintaining more than one SCL is unnecessary duplication of work and waste of resources.

Most of the State Acts and Model bills drafted, designate the biggest public library existing in the State as SCL and adopts it to the system and shares its resources among participating units. But instead of designating Trivandrum Public Library the oldest and biggest collection in the State as SCL the KPLA deems it to be one of the many State libraries it will establish[27]. The Act provides for no SCL in its system. Instead it provides that KSLC shall establish one or more State libraries at such place or places in the State as may be considered necessary[28]. The relation of State libraries with other State libraries and the different level service units and the need for more than one such institution is not defined in the Act.

Library Co-operation

To make the best possible use of the document resources not only in the public library system but also in other types of libraries in the State such as universities, special libraries etc., a system of inter-library co-operation needs to be developed in the State as a whole[29]. It would also be useful and economical if centralization of different aspects such as acquisition programme, technical processing etc. of documents should be introduced at State level or at different levels of the system. The KPLA gives no such provision for co-operation or centralized processing and the institution which is to give leadership in such activities, that is SCL is absent in KPLA.

State Library Service

A State Library Service brings the manpower of the State in one pool and thus avoids the waste of time and money involved in filling up posts; that would otherwise involve if every Local Library Authority were to appoint the staff independently[30]. A State Library Service further avoids the influence of members of the Local Library Authority in day-to-day management of libraries. Mysore Act has created a special State Library Service and it ensures proper administration and economy through State Library Authorities that is DLC and TLU; the powers to appoint and control required officers and servants[31].

Finance

For the growth and development of a public library system in a State, there must be specific provision in the Act for required financial support. Since education is an essential responsibility of a welfare State public library system should obviously be established and maintained at the expense of the State. According to the Model Act of Ranganathan the suitable sources for this purpose are library cess, grants from the State Governments and grants from Central Government. In the provisions related to finance; KPLA accepts all the generally accepted principles. The Act provides that the KSLC shall levy a library cess in the form of surcharge on building tax or property tax collected by local bodies at the rate of five paise for whole rupee[32]. The cess shall be paid to the KSLC by local bodies.

As per the provisions in KPLA the government may also make every year a grant to the KSLC of a sum which shall not exceed one per cent of the budget for education[33]. This amount of grant is insufficient. Ranganathan's Library Development Plan, the documents on National Policy on Library and Information Science and Indian Library Association suggests that six per cent of the Education budget of the State should be set apart for libraries.

The Act also provides for a State Library Fund from which all expenses of KSLC, DLC and TLU shall be met[34]. Grants of State and Central Governments to KSLC, contributions by persons, bodies or authorities to KSLC and other funds transferred to it shall be credited to State Library Fund. KSLC shall distribute from State Library Fund such amounts as required for each DLC and TLU. Against creating such Library funds as suggested by Model Act and some State Acts at State and Local levels; provision of KPLA related to finances providing a centralized fund is truly a notable improvement.

REFERENCES

1. Harish Chandra and Narendra Kumar. Network based public library system. In Biswas, S.C. *Public Library Development Perspectives.* Delhi: ILA, 1985.
2. Ranganathan, S.R. Library development plan: *Thirty year programme for India with draft bills for the union and the constituent states.* Delhi: Delhi University, 1950.
3. Ranganathan, S.R. Model Public libraries Act. 1972. In Ranganathan, S.R. and Neelameghan, A. *Public Library System.* Bangalore: SRET, 1972.
4. Kerala. *Kerala Public Libraries* (Kerala Granthasala Sangham) Act, 1989. Trivandrum: Govt. Press, 1989.
5. Ranganathan. *Op. cit.,* 3. Clause 2.
6. Prasad, H.N. Library legislation in India: A comparative study. In Rout, RK. *Library Legislation in India: Problems and Prospects.* New Delhi: Reliance, 1986.
7. Hewit, AR. Indian public library law. In *Journal of Indian Library Association,* 1962, Vol. 4, Nos. 3-4.
8. Raman Nair, R. Reforms required in Kerala Public Library Act 1989. *ILA Bulletin,* Vol. 28, No. 1-2, 1992.
9. Kerala. *Op. cit.,* 4. Clause 3. Section 1.
10. Karnataka. *Karnataka Public Libraries Act.* 1965. Bangalore: Govt. Press. Clause 3, Section1.
11. Kerala. *Op. cit.,* 4. Clause 8, Section 1, sub-section a to h and Section 2.
12. Raman Nair, R. Gramangalil vijnana vitharanam. Trivandrum: *Vijnanakairali* 1988, Vol. 14, No. 8.
13. Mangala, P.B. Library legislation in India. In Rout. *Library Legislation in India: Problems and Prospects.*

14. Kerala. *Op. cit.,* 4. Clause 3, Section 2.
15. *Ibid.* Clause 3, Section 3.
16. Raman Nair, R. Keralathile granthasala prasthanam. Cochin: *Veekshanam.* 11.8.1987.
17. Mangala. *Op. cit.,* 13.
18. Prasad. *Op. cit.,* 6.
19. Kerala. Legislative Assembly. Proceedings of 21.2.1989. Trivandrum: Govt. Press, 1989.
20. Kerala. *Op. cit.,* 4. Clause 3, Section 5.
21. Kerala. Legislative Assembly. 1989. Proceedings of 8.2.1989. Trivandrum: Govt. Press.
22. *Ibid.*
23. *Ibid.* 21.2.1989.
24. *Ibid.* 3.2.1989.
25. *Ibid.* 9.2.1989.
26. Misra, Jogesh. *History of Libraries and Librarianship in Modern India since 1850.* Delhi: Atma Ram, 1979.
27. Kerala. *Op. cit.,* 4. Clause 8, Section 1, sub-section f.
28. *Ibid.*
29. Mangala. *Op. cit.,* 13.
30. Misra. *Op. cit.,* 26.
31. Kerala. *Op. cit.,* 4. Clause 8. Section 1, Sub-section h, clause 17 Section 1, Sub-section h. and clause 25, Section 1, sub-section h.
32. *Ibid.* Clause 48.
33. *Ibid.* Clause 30.
34. *Ibid.* Clause 32.

14

LESSONS TO BE LEARNED

The analysis of the people's library movement in Kerala as well as the Kerala Public Libraries (Kerala Granthasala Sangham) Act 1989 which is a fruit of the movement are based on the hypothesis that:

* Information is a basic resource for national development[1];
* Information plays significant role in improving literacy rate, educational standard and quality of research;
* Information helps to throw of social maladies from the minds of the people;
* Cultivation of natural and industrial resources and the development of human resources; its prior correlative requires continuous dissemination of latest scientific ideas and information among one and all[2];
* Information is a must for the successful functioning of democratic governments, for it enables individuals organizations and government to take informed decisions;
* Every citizen must have the right to obtain the information he needs irrespective of his physical, social and economic condition from the national stores of information;
* It is the primary duty of a democratic government to make the nation's whole information resource easily accessible and freely available to all;
* An efficient and continuous sharing of the basic resource that is information which is required in a socialist set-up can be ensured only by a public library legislation[3].

Right to Information

Our country has a considerable stock of information resources in its libraries and other institutions located at different places. They are continuously acquiring more resources from inside and outside the country. Collection and organization of information in all forms and formats and the dissemination of it to the people are the primary function of libraries especially public libraries. So, as Public Library Research group has described; public library system contributes to sustaining the quality of life in all its aspects—educational, economic, industrial, scientific and cultural—and promotes the concept of a democratic society in which equal opportunity exists for all to develop into true citizens, with whole and balanced personalities leading to an increase in the sum total of the man's happiness and awareness of himself, his fellowmen and his environment[4]. So the government must take appropriate step to maintain and develop this sector which is collecting, organizing and disseminating information so as to make them easily and freely accessible to all.

To ensure every man's right to information, public libraries should pool the total resources of the State and nation and should make it available to all the people in an unbiased and efficient way[5]. These functions cannot be fulfilled by isolated libraries or library systems limited within localities or States. A library system should have National Library at the apex with each State having its State Central Library and a network of public library services with District and Taluk Central Libraries and service outlets at village levels[6]. A system of co-operation and co-ordination would be established between all types of libraries with the ultimate aim that any one living anywhere should have access to the document and information resources of the State, the country and even the whole world at a time when he requires them and in a form which would best suit his needs[7].

In order that this may be done as fully, promptly, cheaply and conveniently as feasible it is necessary to establish an efficient system at national level with State Systems as participating units. These systems should be under the authority of law at national and State levels and should be well co-ordinated and backed by efficient administrative machineries; the Ministries and Directorates formed on the basis of legislation to implement policy decisions.

Network for Information Flow

If the information resources of the entire nation is to form a single unit with an indefinite mobility to move from end to end of the nation, so as to make the resources useful to all those residing in different States, the States should have uniform library and information systems supported by law. Without the States having a uniform pattern of library system and legislation, co-ordination at the national level and sharing of resources will not be practicable[8]. Of the 25 States and 7 union territories only 9 have library legislation now. But the existing legislations were not uniform and the working of most acts show that the systems envisaged by them are not efficient. Without learning lessons from other Acts or considering the advances and growth in the information sector, Kerala also has enacted a legislation which is not at all useful for information service to the people. Its system cannot become a participating unit of a National Library and Information System which will be founded on scientific methods. More States will pass such defective legislation and more they do, the longer it will take to bring them into line and materialize the objectives of National Library and Information service.

Legislation for Information Service

The fault is not that of Kerala or other States only. It is also due to the wrong policy of the centre. Library legislation requires mandatory legislation. In 1947 Ranganathan has advised for a National Library System and Union Library Act at the Centre and State Library Act for States which can enforce a uniform pattern at secondary level[9]. In 1957 Sinha Committee also recommended a Union Library Act by Government of India and State Library Act by each State[10]. But no action has been taken by Central Government on this line. The longer the Central Government hesitate to enact a Central Act and insist on mandatory State legislation the more difficult it will be to provide this basic service, and materialize the National Library and Information System as recommended by Chattopadhyaya Committee[11].

One reason for the inactivity of Central Government is the existing constitutional and legal hindrances. In Constitution, libraries fall under State list as a subject coming under the jurisdiction of State Governments. So now States only can enact legislation on public library system. Formerly Education was also under State List. But when Government of India faced problems in the management of education system it amended the Constitution by Constitution 42nd Amendment Act 1976 and changed education from State List to Concurrent List[12]. If by such an amendment Act Libraries which are the inseparable part of education also can be changed to concurrent list on which Central Government and State Government can legislate; it will solve the problem of public library legislation in India in a single stroke permanently[13]. It will ensure the uniform, systematic and speedy establishment and development of network of public libraries in the country as required by National Library and Information Dissemination System.

Union and State Library Acts

For being co-ordinated at the national level it is essential that the central government should enforce by the provisions of the Union Library Act; a uniform pattern for library systems of the States. Centre should also prepare and provide a Model Act to be used by the States. Whatever the size of the State, if the Act follows the State administrative system at different levels; the service point of the lowest viable unit will have to serve almost the same size of the population in every region of India.

The latest of the Model Act was drafted years back. In course of the years some provisions would have become outdated in their essential features. Then the observation of the working of the existing Acts also can suggest some alterations and additions in the Model Act. it is therefore urgent that the Government of India appoints a committee with specified time limit to conduct a study of the Model Act and working of the existing State Acts and to frame a Model State Act which is to be used for State legislation. Till this committee submits its report the State Governments may be directed to desist from enacting any defective legislation. This is essential to eliminate wastage of energy, money and materials which is bound to happen especially where the methods of trial and error and hit or miss are still followed as in Kerala instead of pursuing rational, real and tried systems.

Amendments Required for KPLA

The evaluation of the KPLA 1989 has vindicated that it has certain serious deficiencies which will detain the library system of Kerala from becoming an active part of the National Library and Information System and from serving the people efficiently and at less cost. To make the system envisaged by KPLA able to play effectively its intended role of collecting, organizing and disseminating information to the people; the following amendments and additions to the Act are suggested.

Instead of providing for a State Library Authority and Library Advisory Committee the KPLA provides only for a Kerala State Library Council (KSLC) but has not named it as State Library Authority. KPLA should clearly lay down who or what should be State Library Authority. So far as it may be possible, the supreme authority should be vested in one individual instead of vesting it in a large committee[14]. Dispersal of power at the top is generally, detrimental to efficiency and service. As provided in the Model Act and latest library Acts of the world, the KPLA may vest such an authority in the Minister of Education.

Representation in KSLC

The KSLC may be given the functions of advising and assisting the SLA as provided by the Model Act. KSLC should be made adequately representative and comprehensive in scope so as to include all interests and shades of opinions as a result of which the rich experience of the cream of the State can be put at the disposal of the authority. Adequate representation of Library and Information Science experts in KSLC is essential for the proper planning and organization of the system. Among its members it should include the Minister as ex-officio Chairman, Director of Public Libraries as ex-officio Secretary, State Librarian, Secretary to Higher Education, Heads of the Departments of Library and Information Science and also librarians of the universities of the State, representative from Library Association of the State, Secretaries of Kerala Sahitya Academy, Sangeetha Nataka Academy, Kerala Lalita Kala Academy and adequate number of members from Kerala Legislative Assembly. Like this necessary additions and amendments may be made in provisions related to Local Library Authorities and Councils.

State Central Library

The Act should provide for the State Central Library. Trivandrum Public Library the biggest Library in the State may be designated as the State Central Library by the Act to make its rich collection useful to the people living throughout the State. The clauses in the KPLA providing for the establishment of more than one library like Trivandrum

Public Library may be removed.

The State Central Library may be charged with the responsibilities of being a depository for all publications brought out in Kerala, publishing Kerala State Bibliography, undertaking centralized processing of documents, working as a centre for inter-library loan within and outside the State, preparing union catalogue of holdings of various libraries of the State, organising a reference collection on different aspects of Kerala, maintaining a strong reference collection and service on general topics and acting as the coordinating agency and source of all technical and other information asked for by the district and other libraries of the State. Layout of the library system of the State with State Central Library, District Central Library and service units at different levels and their relation with each other unit or authority should be spelled out in KPLA.

Administrative Machinery

The Act should provide for State Library Service. All personnel working in the different public library systems as now provided by KPLA should be brought into a single State service. All posts in the Department of Public Libraries, the State Central Library and in all libraries maintained by Local Library Authorities should be filled by appointment of persons belonging to State Library Service. For the implementation of the policies and decisions taken by State Library Authority, KPLA should provide for proper and adequate administrative machinery. It should provide for a separate Department of Libraries which shall be headed by a professionally qualified Director. The Act should also provide for a professionally qualified person as State Librarian who will be having the status of an additional Director in the Department.

The State Library service shall also consist District Librarians, Taluk Librarians, Village Librarians and such other classes and categories of posts as the Government may from time to time determine. All members of the said service should be Government servants, and their recruitment and conditions of service shall subject to the provision of Article 309 of Constitution of India be regulated by such rules as may be prescribed.

Knowledge explosion and the enormous quantity of printed materials and other recorded information flooding every day, requires highly specialized staff to evaluate and collect the required recorded information and to do the quick and timely dissemination of required information to the user. It is the knowledge, skill, initiative and character of the personnel who handle this work which determines the extent to which the information resources becomes useful to the public. It is the quality of workforce that will determine the quality of services which the public library system can offer.

In order to ensure proper library and information service to the people the law should lay down the minimum professional qualification for the posts of Director of Libraries, State Librarian, District Librarian, Taluk Librarian and various kinds of other library jobs. Further proper cadres of library staff should be provided by the law on the pattern of other professions and civil services.

Standards and Finance

Public library standards are essential to the effectiveness of public library systems and without them libraries cannot offer the best service to users. The KPLA should clearly lay down as to whether the library authorities are bound legally to provide standard and adequate library service. The world trend today is towards making it obligatory upon the library authorities to provide library service to the people of their respective areas. Library authorities should be obliged to conform to standards of library service as laid down by central government or other appropriate agency.

In order to increase the range of the resources of public libraries and meet the needs of the users; various forms of inter-library cooperation will be required particularly in the area of reference and information services. No single service outlet can meet all information requirements of the community it serves; from what is stored in that unit only. In view of this, provisions for resource sharing and networking should be included in the law.

Universal diffusion of knowledge among the people is highly conducive to the preservation of their freedom, a greater equalization of their social advantages, their industrial success and their physical intellectual and moral advancement and elevation[15]. Public library and information system is the only system which can undertake the dissemination of knowledge effectively, conveniently and economically for the benefit of all the citizens. It is the only system that is accessible also to the 75 per cent of the population who cannot successfully approach the formal educational institutions or huge special information stores maintained away from them[16]. Considering this aspect of public library system it is only just that 15 per cent of the amount allotted for education in State budget be earmarked for the library system. The present one per cent is too meagre to maintain such an important and costly system.

Coverage and Language

There is a trend in modern legislation to include in the statutory law, only minimum number of factors and leave the other factors to the care of the administrative legislation. However this trend is dangerous, especially in the case of social legislation of which; the benefits are not direct. The public being not sensitive, bureaucracy may not handle the administrative legislation with proper care[17]. Ranganathan considers administration also as one of the important factors to be provided for in library legislations[18]. The KPLA should also provide matters of administrative detail. The Act may be perverted unless the form of administration was also not provided in the Act. Any surreptious subversion of an Act can be prevented by putting detailed provision in the Act itself, so that they might not be encroached upon without amending the Act[19]. Smooth working of an infant system might be jeopardised unless the legislation supporting it mentions in detail things which are usually left to ordinary legislation in Acts related to established systems.

The language of the Act should also be made more clear and unambiguous. Standard terminology of Library and Information Science should be used to denote the materials and processes in library system. In this regard A.R. Hewit observes: Indian library legislation, both existing and recommended needs to be simplified and made less ambiguous[20].

Trend against Reform

An immediate amendment to KPLA which rectifies all the defects pointed out above, is required if KPLA is to enable an effective library and information system. The objections against these suggestions that may be put forward by the persons and movement that worked behind the present legislation is that appointing the Minister as State Library Authority, or constituting a body with experts, government officials and Minister also in it, as SLA or advisory council will make the system less democratic and more bureaucratic. During the clause-wise discussions of the Kerala Public Library Bill 1989 in the Kerala

Legislative Assembly Sri T.M. Jacob the ex-Education Minister who prepared the Kerala Public Library Bill 1985 pointed out the serious defect of the present Bill. According to him it is not advisable to provide for a non-official who is the elected Secretary of KSLC to do the appropriation of the annual funds of about 10 crore allotted for library and information service[21]. The person requires continuity of his office and so the Secretary of the council should be an official not below the rank of a Government Joint Secretary[22]. But the suggestions were not accepted and Education Minister Sri K. Chandra Sekaran who piloted the Bill told that the difference of KPLA with the other Acts is that it envisages a purely democratic set-up for libraries and so people should administer the system[23].

But the experience on this line has shown against recommending such a system. The findings of Ashok Mehta Committee and Committees appointed by various State Governments to study the cause of failure or partial success of elected bodies should be an eye opener to the protagonists of this system for library and information services[24]. All the reasons attributed by these committees to elected bodies; political factionalism developing and diluting efficient working, misappropriation of funds and lack of direct attention by Government are all applicable to this system too. Can a very important system of the State which is to organise the basic resource required for the development in all aspects of life and to distribute that efficiently and equally among one and all; afford to sustain such serious defects and risk, in its system?

Democratic Set-up

Arguments vindicating the baselessness of considering an elected body of library members; a more democratic Library Authority than a Minister; has appeared in the press while the Bill was under preparation. If the system is to be truly democratic it should be a system run by the representatives of all the people for whom it is intended. The expected users of a public library system is the whole population. So it is the representatives of the whole population that should administer it. But the KSLC is constituted not with such representation but with representation of library members only. The members of public libraries are less than 5 per cent of the population and they belong to the group of educated and socially advanced persons or class which comes to only 20 per cent of the population. But the system is not intended for them only nor paid for its maintenance only by them. It belongs to the whole population. So limiting the right of electing the representatives who are to run the machinery, within the members is in no way justifiable[25]. Members are in a position to evaluate criticise and reform the system; but have no right to limit its administration within them.

If the whole population of the State is to exercise their power the State Library Authority is to be responsible to the legislature which is elected on adult franchise and which is having representation of all the people. So the Minister for Education or for Libraries if there is one, being the SLA, advised by a council consisting of experts on the system and required number of members elected through different levels of the library system is the most advisable set-up in a democracy. Simply organizing the Library system in a democratic way has got no meaning if the system cannot achieve its aim to the full. The system is not for system's sake. Public library system is not a system for training the people in the working of democratic systems as people's library movement and its leaders claims it to be. It is also not a system to give people, entertainment or a stage for mere cultural activities. In these days it is to be a highly specialized system which makes for the people the access to information easy and free. Public library system is potentially a means of establishing some measure of equal access to, and redistribution of, the wealth of information[26]. How freely and how equally citizens have access to knowledge determines how equally they can share in the governing of our society and in the work and rewards of our economy.[27]

REFERENCES

1. Raja Rammohan Roy Library Foundation. *National Policy on Library and Information System.* Culcutta: the author, 1985.
2. Ranganathan, S.R. Philosophy of free book service for all. In Ranganathan, S.R., Ed. *Free Book Service For All:* An international survey. Bombay: Asia, 1968.
3. Usherwood, Bob. *The Public Library as Public Knowledge.* London: Library Association, 1989.
4. Heeks, P and Turner, P., Ed. *Public Library: Aims and Objectives.* London: Public Libraries Research Group; 1981.
5. Raman Nair, R. Gramathinte Hridayam. Trivandrum: *Granthalokam,* December 1985.
6. Raman Nair, R. Bharatha Desiya Granthalayam: Oravalokanam. Trivandrum: *Vijnanakairali,* 1989, Vol. 20, No. 10.
7. Mangala, P.B. Library legislation in India. In Rout, R.K. *Library Legislation in India: Problems and Prospects.* New Delhi: Reliance, 1986.
8. Raman Nair, R. Gramangalil Vijnana vitaranam. Trivandrum: *Vijnanakairali,* 1988, Vol. 19, No. 8.

9. Ranganathan, S.R. Library development plan: Thirty Year Programme for India with Draft Bills for the Union and the Constituent States. Delhi: Delhi University, 1950.
10. India, Education and Youth Services, Ministry of -, Libraries, advisory Committee for, Chairman: K.P. Sinha, Report. New Delhi: Govt. of India, 1959.
11. India, Education and Culture, Ministry of -, National Policy of Library and Information system, Committee on -, Chairman: Chattopadhyaya. Report. New Delhi: GOI, 1986.
12. Basu, Durga Das. *Introduction to the Constitution of India.* New Delhi: Prentice Hall, 1989.
13. Bansal, G.S. and Tikkoo, U.K. New perspectives of library legislation for India: A proposal. In Biswas, S.C., Ed. *Public Library Development Perspectives.* New Delhi: ILA, 1985.
14. Ranganathan, S.R. Library legislation and its facets *Library Herald,* 1959, Vol. 1, No. 4.
15. Massachusetts. An act to authorise encourage and ensure the formation increase and perpetuation of public libraries, 1851. Massachusetts: Govt. Press.
16. Raman Nair. *Op. cit.,* 8.
17. Misra, Jogesh. *History of Libraries and Librarianship in Modern India since 1850.* New Delhi: Atma Ram, 1979.
18. Ranganathan. *Op. cit.,* 14.
19. Basu, *Op. cit.,* 12.
20. Hewit, A.R. Indian public library law in *Journal of Indian Library Association.* 1962, Vol. 4, Nos. 3-4.
21. Kerala Legislative Assembly. Proceedings. 9th February 1989.Trivandrum: Government Press, 1989.
22. *Ibid.*
23. *Ibid.*
24. Hashmi, Syed Ali. Library legislation in India. In ILA conf. papers. New Delhi: ILA, 1983.
25. Raman Nair, R. Kerala Granthasala Niyamam: Chila prarambha chinthakal. Cochin: *Veekshanam:* 14, 8. 1987.
26. Usherwood. *Op. cit.,* 3.
27. American Library Association. *Freedom and Equality of Access to Information.* Chicago: ALA, 1986.

BIBLIOGRAPHY

Achutha Menon. *Cochi rajyacharitham.* Calicut: Mathrubhoomi, 1989.

American Library Association, Public Library Association, Standards Committee. Minimum standards for public library system. Chicago: ALA, 1966.

American Library Association. Freedom and Equality of Access to Information. Chicago:ALA. 1986.

American Library Association. Minimum Standards for Public Library Systems. New York: ALA, 1966.

Basu, Durga Das. *Introduction to the Constitution of India.* New Delhi: Prentice Hall. 1989.

Bhaskara Panikkar, P.T. Granthasala Niyamam Inganeyo? *Kerala Kaumidhi,* 3.10.1985.

Bipin Chandra. *Modern India.* New Delhi: NCERT, 1971.

Butler, Pierce. *An Introduction to Library Science:* Chicago: Phoenix, 1933.

Campbell, H.C. *Developing Public Library Systems and Services:* Paris: UNESCO. 1983.

Cashmore, H.M. In his forward to Norris. D.M. *History of Cataloguing.* London:Grafton, 1939.

d'Olier, J.H. and Delmas, B. *Planning National Infrastructure for Documentation, Libraries and Archieves.* Paris: UNESCO, 1975.

Damodaran, K. and Narayana Pillai, C. *Keralathile Swatantriya Samaram.* Trivandrum: KBS, 1958.

Downs, Robert B. Resorces for Research in Librarianship. *Library Trends.* 1964, 13, 6-14.

Gardner, Frank M. *Public Library Legislation: A Comparative Study.* Revised and updated by H.C. Campbell, Paris: UNESCO, 1978.

Gopinathh, M.A. History of library legislation in India. In Ranganathan, S. R. Ed. *Public Library System,* Bangalore: SREL, 1972.

Gopinatha Rao, Ed. *Travancore Archeological Series.* Vol. I, Trivandrum: Government Press, 1947.

Granthasala Sangham. Resolutions passed by various Taluk Library Unions of Kerala Grathasala Sangham published in its *Journal Granthalokam* during October, November and December, 1960.

Hashmi, Syd Ali. Library Legislations in India. In ILA Conference papers. New Delhi: ILA, 1983.

Heeks, P. and Turner, P. (ed.) *Public Library : Aims and Objectives:* London: Public Library Research Group: 1981.

Hessel, Alfred, A History of Libraries, Translated by Reuben Peiss, Washington: Scare Crow, 1977.

Hewit, A.R. Indian public library law in *Journal of Indian Library Association.* 1962, Vol. 4, Nos. 3-4.

Hook, H.T. The organization of library systems and the example of Britain. In Canadian Library Association's Conference Proceedings. Ottawa: CL4, 1974.

India, Information and Broadcasting, Ministry of India: a reference annual 1987, New Delhi.

India, Education and Youth Services, Ministry of Libraries, Advisory Committee for Chairman: K.P. Sinha, Report. New Delhi: Govt. of India, 1959. 11. India Education and Culture, Ministry of National Policy of Library and Information system, Committee on, Chairman: Chattopadhyaya. Report. New Delhi: GOI, 1986.

India, Education and Youth Services, Ministry of—, Libraries, Advisory Committee for—,Report. New Delhi: the author, 1957.

India. *Census of India* 1989. Series 10. Kerala. New Delhi: Publications Division, 1989.

Kaufman, Paul. Some community libraries in eighteenth century Europe: A reconnaissance *Libri.* 1972, 22, 1-57.

Kaula, P.N. Some facts about library legislation in India. In Rout, *Library Legislation in India.*

Kerala Granthasala Sangham. Granthasala manual. Trivandrum: the author, 1967.

Kerala Granthasala Sangham. Constitution and Rules. Trivandrum: the author, 1975.

Kerala Legislative Assembly. Proceedings. 9th February 1989. Trivandrum: Government Press, 1989.

Kerala Legislature, Public Libraries Bill, Select Committee on, Chairman: Mohammed Koya, C.H. Report, Trivandrum: Government Press, 1977.

Kerala Legislature. Kerala Public Library Bill 1985: Background materials. Trivandrum: the author, 1986

Kerala Legislature. Kerala Public Library Bill 1971: Background materials. Trivandrum: The Author, 1972.

Kerala Legislature. Kerala Public Libraries Bill 1977, Trivandrum, Government Press, 1977.

Kerala Legislature: Kerala Public Libraries Bill 1971. Trivandrum: Government Press, 1971.

Kerala Legislature, Public Libraries Bill, subject Committee on, Chairman, Chandrasekharan, K. Report. Trivandrum: Government Press, 1989.

Kerala, Keral Public Library *(Kerala Granthasala Sangham)* Bill 1989. Trivandrum: Govt. Press, 1989.

Kerala Government Orders. Ms No. 429. Edn.: Dtd. 25.7.1961, RL No. 843/66/Edn. dtd. 30.3.1966, 25198/43/67 Edn, dtd. 9.7.1969. RJ No. 1186 Edn. dtd. 4.8.1971, RJ No. 375/76/H Edn. dtd. 21.2.1976 and MS No. 39/81/H. Edn. dtd. 9.3.1989.

Kerala Public Relations, Dept. of Press in Kerala : a useful summar, Trivandrum: Government Press, 1977.

Kunjan Pillai, Elamkulam, P.N. *Samskarathinte Nazhikakullukal.* Kottayam: NBS. 1960.

——, *Studies in Kerala History,* Kottayam: NBS, 1970.

Leign, Robert D. Repot of the public library inquiry. New York: Columbia, 1956.

Line, Maurice B. Lines of thought: Selected Papers. London: Clive Bingley. 1988.

Mangala, P.B. Library legislation in India. In Rout, R.K. *Library Legislation in India: Problems and Prospects.* New Delhi: Reliance 1986.

Mani, C.K. Twenty-five years of progress, Kerala Granthasala Sangham 1945-1970. In papers of 27th State Conference of the Sangham. Kottayam: KGS, 1972.

Massachusetts. An Act of authorise encourage and ensure the formation increase and perpetuation of public libraries, 1851. Massachusetts: Govt. Press.

Memorandum submitted to Government by Kerala Granthasala Sangham published in *Granthalokam,* November, 1960.

Misra, Jogesh. *History of Libraries and Librarianship in Modern India since 1850.* New Delhi: Atma Ram, 1979.

Mukherjee, A.K. *Librarianship: Its Philosphy and History.* Bombay Asia, 1966.

Murison, W.J. *Public Library: Its Origin Purpose and Significance,* Ed. 3. London: Clive Bingley, 1988.

Namboodiripad, E.M.S. *Keralam Malayalikalude Mathrubhoomi.* Trivandrum: Chinta, 1969.

Narayana Pillai, C. Dr. S.R. Ranganathan report. Trivandrum: *Granthalokam,* September, 1960.

Nilakanta Sastri, K.A. *History of South India from Prehistoric times to present.* London: OUP, 1959.

Norris, D.M. *History of Cataloguing.* London, Grafton, 1939.

Olle, James G. *Library History.* London: Clive Bingley, 1967.

Panikkar, P.N. (Ed.) *Keralathile Granthasala Prasthanam,* Trivandrum: Steps, 1982.

- —, Granthasala Prasthanathe Sarkar Takarkaruthu. Trivandrum: *Kerala Kaumudhi,* 26.6.1985.

— —, Library movement in Kerala. *Herald of Library Science,* 1974, Vol. 13. No. 3-4

Parameshwaran Nair. *Malayala Sahitya Charitram.* Kottayam: Spcs, 1973.

Public Library Research Group and Library Association. Purpose of Public Libraries. *Library Association Record,* 1971, Vol. 73, No. 12.

Rajaram Mohun Roy Library Foundation. National Policy on Library and Information System. Calcutta: The author, 1984.

Ramachandran Nair, Adoor, K.K. Kerala State gazetter. Trivandrum: State Gazetters, 1986. Vol. 2. Part I.

Ramakrishnan Nair. Constitutional experiements in Kerala. Trivandrum: The Author, 1964.

Raman Nair, R. Attaniyillattavaunm arivu Pakaran. Trivandrum: *Kerala Patrika.* 24.11.1986.

— —, Emergence of organised library movement in Kerala. *International Library Movement.* Vol. 14, No. 2, 1992..

— —, R. Gramathinte Hridayam. Trivandrum: *Grantha Lokam.*

December, 1985.

——, Gramangalil Vijnanavitaranam. Trivandrum: *Vijnanakairali,* 1988, Vol. 14, No. 8.

——, Granthasala Niyamam: Samuhya Vidhya-Bhayasathinte Adittara. Cochin: *Veekshanam,* 22.11.86.

——, Keralathile granthasala Prasthanam. Cochin: *Veekshanam,* 11.8.1987.

——, Kerala Granthasala Sangham Lakshyam Nediyo? Cochin: *Veekshanam,* 12.8.1987.

——, Kerala Granthasala Niyamam: Chila parambha cinthakal. Cochin: *Veekshanam,* 14.8.1987

——, Nature and use of library history. In *Library Movement and Library Development in India,* New Delhi, ILA, 1994.

——, Origins of people's Library movement in Kerala. *Granthana,* Vol. 7, No. 1, 1994.

——, Public Library system in Ancient South India. *ILA Bulletin,* Vol. 12, No. 3.

——, Public library development in Kerala: a historical perspective. Prceedings of South Indian History Congress. Dharwad, Karnataka University, 1992.

——, *Public Library Development.* New Delhi, Ess Ess, 1994.

Ramanujan Nair, R. *Library Movement in Kerala.* Trivandrum: Writers Club, 1974.

Ranganathan, S.R. Library legislation and its facets. *Library Heralad,* 1959, Vol. 1. No. 4.

——, Library development plan: Thirty Year Programme for India with Draft Bills for the Union and the Constituent States. Delhi: Delhi University, 1950.

——, *Free Book Service for All: An International Survey.* Bombay: Asia, 1968.

——, Library development plan with a draft library bill for Kerala State. Trivandrum: Government, Press, 1960.

Public Library system and human sources. *Herald of Library Science,* 1967, Vol. 6, No. 4.

Savage, E.A. In his introduction to Thornton, John L. *Chronology of Librarianship,* London: Grafton, 1941.

Sreedhara Menon. *A Survey of Kerala History.* Kottayam: SPCS, 1976.

——, (Ed.) A. Kerala District Gazetteers: Trivandrum. Trivandrum: Government Press, 1962.

— —, (ed.) Kerala District Gazetteers: Trivandrum. Trivandrum: Government Press, 1962.

Sreeraj, B. Kakshi rastreeyam takartha oru mahaprasthanam. Calicut: *Mathrubhoomi Weekly,* 26.6.1982.

Surendran, S.K. Granthasala Samkamillatta Granthasala Bill venda. *Kerala Kaumudhi,* 12.12.1985.

Syed Ali Hashmi, Library legislation in India in ILA Conference Papers, New Delhi, ILA, 1983.

Thompson, James. *History of Principles of Librarianship.* London: Clive Bingley, 1977.

Thornton, John L. Selected Readings in the history of librarianship London: Library Association 1966.

Tofler, Alvin. *Third Wave,* New York, NAL, 1985.

Travancore, All Travancore Library Association, Committee on—Report. Trivandrum; the author, 1948.

Travancore-Cochin. Government Order No. M 98 dtd. 5.2.1958.

Trivandrum Public Library. Administration report. Trivandrum. Government Press. 1981.

UNESCO and IFLA. UNESCO Public Library Manifesto. Paris: UNESCO. 1972.

UNESCO. Establishing a legislative framework for the implementation of NATIS. Paris: UNESCO, 1977.

United Kingdom, Education, Board of-, Public Libraries, Committee on, Report, London: HMSO, 1927.

Usherwood, Bob. The Public library as public knowledge. London: Library Association, 1989.

Velu Pillai, T.K. *Travancore State Manual.* Trivandrum: Government Press. 1947.

INDEX